MW01143111

SeaKayak

Paddling
through
History
Vancouver
& Victoria

Sea Kayak
Paddling
through
History
Vancouver
& Victoria

Aileen Stalker
Andrew Nolan

To Mom and Dad/Grandma and Grandpa,
who encouraged a love of history and learning

Rocky
Mountain Books
Calgary–Victoria–Vancouver

We acknowledge the financial support of the Government of Canada through the Book Publishing Industry Development Program (BPIDP) and the support of the Alberta Foundation for the Arts for our publishing program.

Printed in Canada

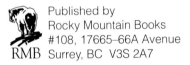
Published by
Rocky Mountain Books
#108, 17665–66A Avenue
Surrey, BC V3S 2A7

Library and Archives Canada Cataloguing in Publication

Stalker, Aileen, 1944-
    Sea kayak Paddling through history: Vancouver & Victoria /
        Aileen Stalker and Andrew Nolan.

Includes index.
ISBN 1-894765-57-5

    1. Sea kayaking--British Columbia--Vancouver Metropolitan Area--Guidebooks. 2. Sea kayaking--British Columbia--Victoria Metropolitan Area--Guidebooks. 3. Vancouver Metropolitan Area (B.C.)--Guidebooks. 4. Victoria Metropolitan Area (B.C.)--Guidebooks. I. Nolan, Andrew, 1979- II. Title.

GV776.15.B7S718 2005   797.122'4'0971133   C2005-901248-X

Contents

Acknowledgements

A writing job that started as helping the guides at Ecomarine Kayaks on Granville Island to have more historical information for their local guided tours, turned into a book! The hours spent reading local history has enriched my appreciation of both the First Nations culture and contributions in the areas of Vancouver and Victoria and the struggles the settlers faced when they first arrived. This book does not pretend to have an in-depth presentation of all the history of the areas in which the paddling trips occur. Instead we concentrated on what could be seen (or had disappeared) when looking at the areas from the water perspective. With a few exceptions, we used a time frame up to the 1920s. I thank the authors listed in the bibliography and the archivists for all of their original research, encouragement and knowledge that helped provide the facts, stories, pictures and anecdotes in this book. A big hug for my co-author and son Andrew, who patiently paddled many of the trips with me and contributed his kayaking knowledge to the maps, trip preparation, resources and contacts, distances, cautions, directions and editing. Thanks also to Stephanie for help with editing, to sister Deb for editing and puppy-sitting and wiping up puddles while I paddled, and to my paddling companions who encouraged me throughout and were a captive audience to my testing the information on our trips: Lorelei, Jean, Nikki, Sabina, Wendy and the Ecomarine crew. A special thanks to RMB associate publisher David Finch and editor Joe Wilderson for guiding two new authors through a steep learning curve.

—Aileen

Disclaimer

There are inherent risks in sea kayaking. While the authors have done their best to provide accurate information and to point out potential hazards, conditions may change owing to weather and other factors. It is up to the users of this guide to learn the necessary skills for safe paddling and to exercise caution in potentially hazardous areas. Please read the introduction to this book, and in particular study the Trip Rating guidelines on pages 8 and 9.

Paddlers using this book do so entirely at their own risk and the authors and publishers disclaim any liability for injury or other damage that may be sustained by anyone using the access and/or paddling routes described.

Introduction

The waters surrounding Vancouver and Victoria have some of the most spectacular and easily accessible paddling in the world. Within an hour's drive from either city you can be paddling in a bustling downtown harbour or the scenic waters of a glacier-carved fjord. Paddling in the harbour of a large city can give you an entirely new outlook on what you had only known from land. Discovering one urban stream that you never knew existed will no doubt entice you to discover more.

The view from the water is often much different and more dynamic than expected, with previously unnoticed art, wildlife and city views, all brought to light from the slow-paced perspective of a kayak. Seals pop up behind you and water birds of all sorts abound, including the graceful blue herons once common in both cities and now slowly returning.

Having spent years paddling the waters of English Bay and False Creek, we often wondered about the history that surrounded us. Who and what were responsible for shaping the waterfront landscape as it is today? Was it part of a master plan or did it just evolve this way through a hundred years of random events?

With any luck, this book will start to answer some of those questions and lead you to your own discoveries. Following these marine trails, which as it turns out many people in all sorts of watercraft have followed before, you will discover that all of Vancouver's and Victoria's waterways played an important part in shaping the cities and regions as they are today. From the first explorers to today's modern condo developments this book will lead you through the surprising histories of two diverse and ever-evolving areas.

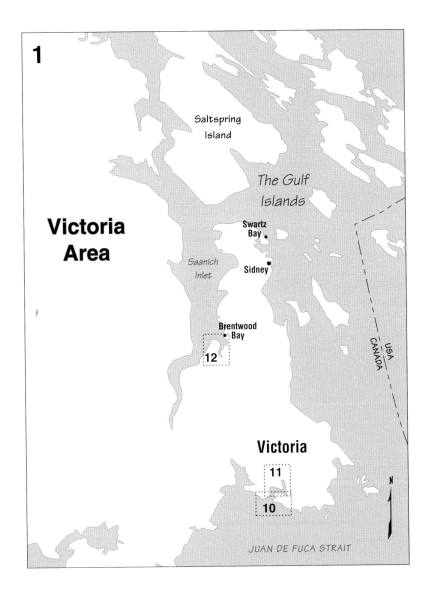

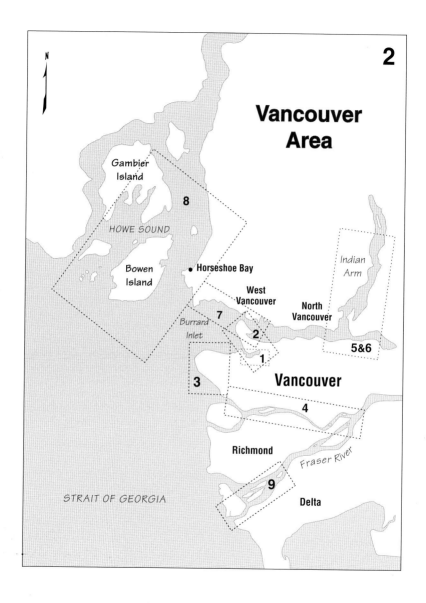

2

Vancouver Area

Gambier Island

HOWE SOUND

8

Bowen Island

• Horseshoe Bay

Indian Arm

West Vancouver

North Vancouver

7

Burrard Inlet

2

1

5&6

3

Vancouver

4

Richmond

Fraser River

9

Delta

STRAIT OF GEORGIA

N

Trip Rating

Routes described in this guide have been rated according to the paddling skills required, normal sea and shoreline conditions, and the level of risk normally associated with such conditions. The rating given to a trip is an indication of what to expect in good, summer conditions. It is an assessment of risk, taking into account paddling skill level and difficulties likely to be encountered.

Difficulty is a measure of sea conditions such as wind, waves, currents, tide rips and length of open-water crossings; and shoreline conditions such as surf and infrequent and/or difficult landings.

Risk is the possibility of inconvenience, discomfort, injury or even loss of life. For the paddler, the level of risk is not constant. Along the same route and with the same paddling conditions, different paddlers will encounter different levels of risk. For a beginner, risky conditions may include small wavelets that arise before white-capped waves appear. For a more skilled paddler the same waves may hardly be noticeable. Risk can be reduced by good paddling skills, knowledge and judgment. Risk increases in worsening conditions, remote locations and with poor decision-making.

There is a complex relationship between paddling skills, difficulty and risk. The individual paddler's skill level, the nature of the route, changing weather, and the presence of a competent leader are essential factors in determining the difficulty and risk of a sea kayak journey.

Sound decision-making is critical to the enjoyment and safety of sea kayak touring, and having an experienced leader can often reduce difficulty and risk to acceptable levels. In the company of a skilled leader, a beginner can paddle safely along a coast rated intermediate. With good leadership a large portion of the Gulf Islands coastline is accessible to beginner-level paddlers, and a coastline rated as "advanced" is by no means the sole domain of the advanced paddler.

The rating descriptions below cover many, but not all, of the factors required in assessing difficulty and risk. There may be other factors to be considered such as river outflows, reflected waves, the profile of a surf beach and the limitations of gear and cold water.

The skill levels referred to below correspond to the conditions, i.e., intermediate paddlers have the attributes necessary to travel safely in intermediate conditions.

Trip Rating courtesy Doug Alderson

Novice conditions – minimal risk
- Sheltered locations with stable conditions.
- Wind calm (less than 8 knots); sea state calm to rippled.
- Travel is along shore with abundant easy landing sites.
- Frequent opportunities for communication and road access; assistance is nearby.

A group of novice paddlers can travel safely on day trips along the shore. Poor decisions or misinterpreting changing weather or sea conditions is unlikely to cause harm or significant inconvenience.

Beginner conditions – low risk
- Mostly sheltered locations with stable conditions.
- Light winds (0–11 knots) current (0–0.5 knots); sea state calm to light chop.
- Abundant easy landing sites and short open crossings less than 1.5 nmi (nautical miles).
- Frequent opportunities for communication and access; assistance may be up to an hour away.

A group of beginners can travel safely on day trips. Intermediate paddlers familiar with the area could lead beginners on an overnight trip. Poor decisions or misinterpreting changing weather or sea conditions is likely to cause inconvenience but unlikely to cause harm.

Intermediate conditions – moderate risk
- A complex open-water environment with the potential for moderate change in conditions.
- Moderate winds (12–19 knots); sea state moderate with wind waves near 0.5 m (metre); surf less than 1 m; current less than 3 knots.
- Intermittent landing opportunities with some difficult landing sites; open-water crossings less than 5 nmi.
- Communication may be interrupted; assistance may be more than one hour away.

A group of intermediate paddlers can travel safely on day trips. Advanced paddlers familiar with the area could lead intermediate paddlers on an extended overnight trip. Poor decisions or misinterpreting changing weather or sea conditions is likely to cause great inconvenience, the need for external rescue and possibly personal harm.

Advanced conditions – considerable risk
- Complex open water environment with frequently changing conditions.
- Continuous exposure to wind, swell or current.
- Strong winds (near 20 knots); sea state rough with wind waves near 1 m; surf greater than 1 m or tide rips greater than 3 knots are routine.
- Infrequent landing opportunities with some difficult landing sites; open-water crossings greater than 5 nmi.
- Remote locations where communication can be difficult or unavailable; assistance may be a day or more away.

A mix of intermediate and advanced paddlers can travel safely on day trips. On extended overnight trips all paddlers should have advanced skills. Poor decisions or misinterpreting changing weather or sea conditions is likely to cause personal harm, without the availability of prompt external rescue.

Urban Paddling

Traditionally, sea kayaking has been seen as a sport for people who enjoy extended adventures into the wilderness, packing all their provisions and supplies to weather stormy seas and rainy nights. The recent growth in kayaking has largely been fuelled by the growing number of recreational and day-trip paddlers. Kayak manufacturers have responded by building an excellent selection of inexpensive, stable and comfortable kayaks to fill this new demand. For people without their own boats, a growing number of outfitters are renting kayaks at reasonable prices, on the water at popular paddling spots or at convenient locations nearby.

We chose the routes for this book for two reasons. First, all of them are close to Vancouver or Victoria, and most are accessible by foot, bike or public transit. Second, all of these routes offer a rich local history to capture your imagination.

While the routes are recounted sequentially, from the suggested put-in to the suggested take-out, all of them stand alone as interesting paddling destinations, whether you read the history before, during or after you go.

We suggest reading through the route at least once, along with the maps in this book and your own charts, before you go. Identify the points of interest you don't want to miss, and if you don't see everything, you can catch it on the return trip or the next time you paddle the route.

The beauty of urban paddling in the Pacific Northwest is that just about every type of paddling condition can be experienced, from the sheltered waters of False Creek and Portage Inlet, to the tidal currents of The Gorge Waterway in Victoria, to the surprisingly varied conditions found in English Bay. All year long there are paddling possibilities to be found for any skill level.

All of the routes with the exception of the North Arm of the Fraser River can be paddled by beginners on a calm sunny day, but our ever-changing weather means that being properly prepared and aware of your surroundings will be critical in ensuring a safe and enjoyable paddle.

Trip Preparation

Kayaking is not in itself a dangerous sport. In the Vancouver and Victoria areas alone, thousands of people each year jump in kayaks for the first time with little or no instruction and have an enjoyable time, never coming close to getting into trouble. Nevertheless, the unpredictable nature of West Coast weather and sea conditions means that sooner or later, unprepared paddlers are going to run into problems.

The best way to educate yourself on proper paddling techniques, the easiest way to get in and out of your boat, required safety equipment, rescue techniques and seamanship is to take a lesson from one of the numerous ocean kayak schools in the area. Before signing up, ask whether their instructors are certified by the Canadian Recreational Canoe (and Kayak) Association. This organization has set the standards required for instructors across the country and will ensure

Urban paddling past Burrard and Granville Bridges

that your instructor is of the highest ability.

Once you have taken an initial lesson, don't forget to review and practise the lessons and techniques you have learned. They will not do you any good in an emergency if you have not practised in years.

The following guidelines are intended as a reminder of some of the things one should consider before heading off. They should not be used as your only trip preparation resource. The Additional Reading section at the back of this book suggests a number of other excellent books dedicated to the subjects you should become familiar with before you set off.

Guided trips

Another good way to introduce yourself to sea kayaking, without having to commit to any lessons, is to take a guided tour from one of the numerous tour operators in the vicinity of the routes this book covers. Many of these operators have been in business for years and have dedicated professional guides. Just don't expect them to know any more local history than you will after reading this book

Gear and equipment

Having the right gear, knowing how to use it, and ensuring it is properly adjusted is an essential part of a safe outing. Whether you own your own gear or are renting or borrowing, take the time before each trip to run through your checklist and make sure you have everything you will need. If you are renting, make sure you are provided with all the equipment required by the Coast Guard.

The official list of required gear can be found at www.tc.gc.ca/Boating-Safety/sbg-gsn/canoe.htm and in the gear checklist in this book. Take the time to adjust your rudder pedals, PFD and seat back before you launch. It may be difficult to do so once you are on the water. Make sure the boat fits you and will be comfortable for the three or more hours most of these trips take.

Weather

Check the weather before you go. It may be clear and sunny when you launch, but an approaching weather system can make things dramatically different in a matter of hours. Environment Canada provides continuous marine weather broadcast for the Vancouver and Victoria areas as well as the rest of the coast. The forecasts are updated four times a day and amended if required. These broadcasts will give you the big picture, but keep in mind that local conditions can be affected by the unique terrain and geography of the area. You should therefore always assess the local conditions before you set out and continue assessing them as you paddle. You can obtain these forecasts by calling 604-664-9010 or 604-666-3655 for the Vancouver area and 250-363-6492 or 250-363-6880 in Victoria. Detailed weather forecasts and information are on-line at the Environment Canada website (http://weatheroffice.ec.gc. ca), including marine forecasts, five-day local forecasts, satellite imagery and weather cameras. A VHF radio will also pick up the broadcasts on Channel 21B or on one of the pre-set weather (WX) channels.

Tides and currents

Tides and currents are another major factor to be aware of. It is not uncommon to have to run down the beach to prevent your boat from floating away. While this is usually embarrassing and comical, many paddlers have been caught unaware by the tide and gotten pushed or pulled in the wrong direction while out on the water. Most often this just adds time and effort to your trip as you paddle against an opposing current, but strong tides and currents have also been the main factor in numerous serious incidents where exhausted paddlers have been unable to make sufficient progress in deteriorating weather. Tides, when combined with wind and waves, can be incredibly powerful. It is never a good idea to set off in a direction that will mean you are paddling against the tide or wind on your way back.

Just like the weather, tides need to be checked before you set out. Volume 5 of the Tide and Current Tables covers the Vancouver and Victoria areas. It is published annually by the Canadian Hydrographic Service and is available at most kayak outfitters and marine supply stores. This is the most accurate source of information available. The tides and currents are calculated only for a number of Reference Ports on the coast, such as Point Atkinson or Victoria Harbour. To get a more accurate prediction of the tides in the area in which you will be paddling you can use the Secondary Ports listed in the back of the tables. These will tell you how much time, height or velocity to add to the Reference Port data for a number of additional points. It is also important to remember to

Leaving the city behind

add one hour to the times listed in the tables during daylight saving time, as the times listed are not adjusted in the summer months. Tide and current information is also available on-line at www.waterlevels.gc.ca or through www.charts.gc.ca.

Charts

Always carry a proper marine chart for the area you will be paddling in. The charts produced in Canada are some of the best in the world and are packed full of useful information. Obviously they are indispensable for route finding and navigating, but they also show areas of strong current and have notes where unusual hazards exist.

At the beginning of each trip the available charts of a useful scale are listed. Information on available charts and a list of local chart dealers is available at www.charts.gc.ca.

Clothing

Being properly dressed can make a huge difference in your comfort on the water. Luckily the clothing required for paddling is generally not all that different from what you might wear for other outdoor pursuits. Cotton is to be avoided at all times. It will absorb water like a towel and remain wet and cold for the rest of the day. This is not only uncomfortable but can lead to more serious consequences such as hypothermia.

The clothing you wear will depend greatly on what time of year it is. In the summer it is often possible to wear just a t-shirt and shorts for most of the day, but it is essential to bring along additional layers that you can put on when you stop for a break and start to cool down or if conditions change. Pack some warm layers and a rain jacket close at hand, in a dry bag on your deck or in the cockpit. A lightweight fleece pullover and a highly packable jacket are ideal to put on while on the water. Some fleece tights or good nylon or polyester hiking pants are great for when you get off the water.

Starting with good base layers, more commonly known as long underwear, will make paddling on those less than perfect days much more comfortable. There are many name brand materials available that are made from synthetic materials such as polyester (fleece) or polypropylene

and will keep you warm even if you get them wet. Wool or blends of wool and synthetic materials also have the same properties and may not get as smelly. One set of mid-weight tops and bottoms should be all you need for weekly outings. Don't forget to wear synthetic underwear unless you want a very soggy bum.

If the weather is cool you will want to add a layer or two on your upper body. Here again synthetics are a must, with fleece being the material of choice. It now comes in many weights to meet anyone's needs. Wool sweaters can be substituted here as well. The key is to have a number of layers you can put on and take off throughout the day, as conditions and your temperature change.

If you are going to paddle in the rain, when it can actually be very

Paddling along False Creek looking south

calm and pleasant, a good set of breathable rain gear is usually good enough. Many people will also use highly breathable, packable and water resistant bicycling tops on days when light showers are possible. Specially designed paddling jackets, cut so as not to interfere with the spray skirt are available, as are paddling pants, which are cut to be comfortable while sitting. These will add to your comfort if you are paddling in wet weather, but are not necessary to get started.

Food and water
Don't skimp on the amount of food and water you take along. Kayaking is great because you can pack as much gear and equipment as you need in the hatches of your boat without creating much additional paddling effort. Make the most of this by taking a minimum of 2 to 3 litres of water per person per day. Becoming dehydrated

is easy when you are paddling in the sun, and often, because of the ocean breeze cooling you as you paddle, it goes unnoticed.

In addition to whatever food you are taking for the day, it is a good idea to pack a few extra items such as energy bars or trail mix in case the trip ends up taking longer than expected.

Communication
Having a reliable way to call for assistance if you need it is not that difficult on the routes in this book, as cellular telephones get good reception in most areas. Make sure to store the phone in a watertight container such as a Pelican case or Otter box. Heavy duty zip-lock bags are a great, inexpensive alternative and are also handy if you want to carry the phone in a pocket of your PFD.

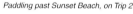

Paddling past Sunset Beach, on Trip 2

Tall ship entering First Narrows, ca. 1917. Photo courtesy West Vancouver Museum & Archives.

A SHORT HISTORY OF THE VANCOUVER AREA

I F THE FIRST PERSON WHO LANDS gets to name the spot, Vancouver should be called Snauq, for the First Nations village that was in the Kitsilano area, or Khwaykhway (whoi-whoi) for the village in Stanley Park, or Narvaez or Galiano after the Spanish captains who sailed along the northwest coast and into what is now called English Bay.

When you are kayaking in English Bay, just imagine that over 3,000 years ago First Nations people paddled in these same waters. The Spanish Captain Narvaez arrived in 1791. In 1792, when two other Spanish explorers, Galiano and Valdes, were lingering around enjoying the

History continues on p. 20

1 False Creek from Granville Island to TELUSphere

Difficulty Novice conditions – minimal risk

Distance 3.5 nmi round trip

Duration 2.5 hours round trip

Charts 3311 Sunshine Coast—Vancouver Harbour to Desolation Sound, 1:40,000
3481 Approaches to Vancouver Harbour, 1:25,000
3493 Vancouver Harbour, Western Portion, 1:10,000

Launching and take-out sites

The easiest place to launch is next to the Kitsilano Point Coast Guard station in Vanier Park. Here you will find a boat ramp and small sand beach. In front of the Maritime Museum there is also a small beach with a sheltered launch site. This is a popular place for people to practise rescue techniques and rolling in the summer. You can also launch from two places on Granville Island: the Ecomarine Ocean Kayak Centre dock and a small dock in Alder Bay near the False Creek Community Centre. If you plan on using the Ecomarine dock, it is a good idea to ask the staff in the store so you do not interfere with their rental operation, especially on weekends in the summer. A little-known launch site is also available in Yaletown. As part of the development of the Expo land, Concord Pacific was required to provide public access to False Creek. There are two publicly accessible small boat launching areas on the east end of the Quayside Marina dock.

Guide **continues on p. 21**

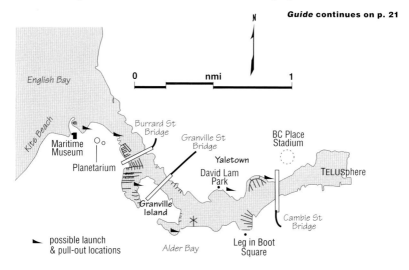

possible launch & pull-out locations

scenery, Captain Vancouver sailed around the point in his boat the *Discovery* and the area became another land claim for Britain.

Captain Vancouver, who had used Spanish maps to find the place, magnanimously gave the name Spanish Banks to the cliffs along English Bay, and some Gulf Islands were given Spanish names for the explorers who sailed among them (e.g., Galiano, San Juan, Lopez, Valdes). However, Captain Vancouver, the British militia and settlers who followed clearly won the naming game.

In the late 1700s both the Spanish and British were in English Bay and exploring Burrard Inlet. Captain Vancouver called it Burrard's Canal after one of his navy friends (it pays to be friends with an explorer), but he did not realize the extent of the body of water it represented.

The peninsula that 100 years later would become Stanley Park was an island at high tide. There were

History **continues on p. 22**

Vancouver looking east from Fairview slopes, ca. 1893.
Photo by Trueman & Caple of Vancouver, courtesy City of Vancouver Archives.

Getting there

Access to this route is not difficult, but may require a good map if you are unfamiliar with the city. Kitsilano Point Coast Guard station, Vanier Park and the Maritime Museum can be accessed from Chestnut Street north of Cornwall Street at the western base of the Burrard Street Bridge. Continue straight north for the Maritime Museum, or, for the Coast Guard station and Vanier Park, turn east on Whyte Avenue just before the Planetarium and Royal Conservatory of Music.

Granville Island is best accessed from 4th Avenue. Heading east, follow the signs that direct you to turn north, immediately passing under the main span of the Granville Street Bridge onto Anderson Street. If heading west, you will turn onto Anderson Street just before the main span of the bridge. There will be a large billboard on your right, often advertising the Public Market. The roads on the Island are all one-way, so proceed with caution if you are unfamiliar with the area.

The Quayside Marina is accessed from Marinaside Crescent, which in turn is accessed by either Davie Street or Drake Street on the south side of Pacific Boulevard in downtown Vancouver. You can also turn off directly from Pacific Boulevard if you are travelling east, just after you pass under the Nelson street on-ramp to the Cambie Street Bridge.

Guide continues on p. 23

Preparing to launch from Granville Island

False Creek from Granville Island to TELUSphere – 21

False Creek looking west to Kitsilano Point, ca. 1890. Granville Bridge is in foreground, Kitsilano Trestle Bridge in background. Photo by Edwards Bros., courtesy City of Vancouver Archives.

water crossings from Burrard Inlet to the head of False Creek, and from Coal Harbour through the present Lost Lagoon to Second Beach. The first-growth Douglas fir trees in the area were over 105 metres tall, and fish and wildlife were abundant. Despite viewing this powerful landscape from the deck of a sailing vessel, apparently no one made the connection between the tall trees and the masts holding up their sails. Instead of seeking lumber, the explorers were almost totally consumed with the fur trade.

It would take another 60 years or so before, in 1859, Captain Richards of the British Navy sailed down the Fraser River from New Westminster into English Bay. His mission was to locate an ocean-based outpost to protect the military camp and growing settlement at New Westminster. There was a perceived threat of an American invasion despite the existence of the Treaty

History continues on p. 24

Parking

Launching from the heart of a large city generally means pay parking. At the Coast Guard station, pay parking is available in the large lot closest to the water, but if you are lucky you may find an empty free spot across from the Vancouver Archives or in front of the Vancouver Museum, which you pass 100–200 m from the water on your way in. There is pay parking available in front of the Maritime Museum. Be careful about parking on the street in the Kitsilano Point area if you are launching from the Maritime Museum, as it is mostly permit parking only.

False Creek

While there are hundreds of free parking spots on Granville Island, securing one for yourself will take some patience. It is not as bad as it seems, though, as spots open up all the time. Just obey the signs. Parking for even a few minutes over the posted time (generally three hours) will result in a ticket. This can be avoided if you park in one of the pay lots or move your vehicle "off island." Parking in Yaletown is probably not recommended, as it is generally metered for a maximum of two hours.

Washrooms

There are washrooms at Ecomarine Ocean Kayak Centre, in Granville Island Public Market (open 8:00 am to 6:00 pm only). There are also Vancouver Parks Board ones to the east of the Coast Guard station, near a coffee shop.

Paddling considerations

False Creek is generally a safe place to paddle, as it is sheltered from strong winds, waves and swell. Caution should be taken especially in the summer months due to the large amount of pleasure boat traffic in the area. While restricted to a maximum speed of 5 knots, the larger party boats can create some steep, choppy waves.

The small Aquabus ferries are generally harmless and are accustomed to small boat traffic in the area. Just be cautious when passing by their docking areas.

Guide continues on p. 25

of 1846, which had established the 49th parallel as an international boundary. (A brief skirmish related to a trespassing pig in 1859 in the San Juan Gulf Islands had reminded the British of undecided property rights that would remain in dispute until 1872.)

Captain Richards was trying to find a water route over to Burrard Inlet, and although in the 1700s there were several shallow high tide crossings from the inlet into the creek, none existed when he sailed in. He was probably not impressed with this, or with the vast mud flats that extended for 5.5 km east at the end of the creek, and so it is said that he named the area False Creek.

He had a bit better luck when he went around the peninsula (Stanley Park) and into Burrard Inlet. Some coal was discovered on the beach, so Coal Harbour and Coal Peninsula were optimistically named.

Coal Peninsula never produced much coal, but it did make a very fine military outpost and became a government military reserve. To provide land access to the area, from 1859–61 a trail was cut from New Westminster through the woods, first to Burrard Inlet (North Road), then to the new settlement called Hastings Mill and on to the military reserve. This secondary road was built in 1860 and followed a First Nations trail. Now named Kingsway (after King Edward VII), it was originally called the New Westminster Road, then Westminster Road.

Maybe it was when all those big trees were cut down to build the roads from New Westminster that someone realized the trees were useful for something other than firewood. The first load of spars left Vancouver for Australia in 1864, and Vancouver became recognized throughout the world for its superb trees.

History continues on p. 26

Some caution should also be taken if you paddle near the various boats anchored in the Creek. Their anchor lines are often complicated messes of scrap metal and cable that would not be enjoyable to get tangled in. Tugs pulling barges still enter the Creek occasionally, heading for the Ocean Construction Supplies plant, and should be given a wide berth.

The route

Heading east from either the Coast Guard station or the Ecomarine dock you will see the large sign for Bridges Restaurant. It is built on the wooden frame from the Atlas Transfer Company, a company that was one of the original industries on this site. The sign and the design of the building represent the intent of planners to showcase the early history of Granville Island's industrial character. The first home of the Emily Carr School of Art and Design used the factory buildings of British Ropes and Westex Manufacturing as part of the buildings on the north part of the Granville Island campus.

You will paddle by Ocean Construction Supplies, which is the last heavy industry remaining on the Island. The buildings have been there since 1914. The company originally provided coal and building supplies, but starting in 1929, they changed to concrete production. Even though getting the company's large trucks on and off Granville Island can be quite the challenge, the Canada Mortgage and Housing Corporation (the Island's landlord) wants to retain this reminder of the Island's industrial past.

The expensive floating homes in Sea Village have gradually replaced the more modest homes that were

Guide continues on p. 27

Burrard and Granville bridges

False Creek from Granville Island to TELUS*phere – 25*

Vancouver, a rough and tough city, grew from a series of small settlements that were given the names Granville, Gastown and Hastings Mill on Burrard Inlet. In April 1886, the population was about 1,000 and the area was officially incorporated as the City of Vancouver.

By then, the city was beginning to develop industries and businesses to supply its increasing population, passing prospectors and the commerce demands of other countries. As well, the city began negotiating for the Canadian Pacific Railway (CPR) to make Vancouver the terminus of the Trans-Canada railway—an event that would prove pivotal to the future of Vancouver.

With the prospects of an exciting future and increased growth, the city burned down on June 13, 1886, destroying the majority of homes and industries.

The next day, the citizens began rebuilding and Vancouver never looked back.

So where did the name Vancouver come from? Well, of course there was that original explorer Captain Vancouver. There is also the story that Canadian Pacific Railway general manager William Van Horne (who was of Dutch ancestry similar to Captain Vancouver) insisted on a name that would be recognized and remembered. Since the CPR owned much of the land in the newly formed city, Mr. Van Horne obviously knew the important principles of real estate marketing: location, location, location and a memorable name.

A TRUE HISTORY OF FALSE CREEK AND GRANVILLE ISLAND

EARLY MAPS INDICATE that it took quite a long time for European explorers to discover False Creek.

When Captain Vancouver entered English Bay in 1792, he did not explore the Creek area or pay atten-

History continues on p. 28

brought to the Creek after they were evicted from Coal Harbour in the 1980s. This was the first legal floating subdivision in Canada.

In the early years of Vancouver, and even until the final eviction in 1955, squatters lived on False Creek in shanties and floating homes. People complained about them, implying they were the cause of an increase in disease and vermin, and that they were "a nest of perverts." This outrage is no longer directed at the houseboat owners, but a similar resentment has been building toward the many small boats moored in the sheltered waters of the Creek. In an attempt to solve the problem, a new Transport Canada regulation in 2004 resulted in a city measure that restricts moorage in the Creek to two consecutive weeks in the summer and three in the winter.

The large mound of earth you will see as you pass the east end of Granville Island is indeed called The Mound. It was made from the torn-up railway ties and construction debris when the island was being redesigned. It is the Island's only spot higher than 10 feet in elevation.

Alder Bay, on the south side of The Mound, once provided passage at high tide around the sandbars between the south shore and the sandbars before the development of Granville Island, when the road approach to the island cut off the waterway. It also provided a sheltered bay for the floating shacks used by workers in the city and in the industries surrounding the Creek, before their eviction.

Several tall buildings will catch your eye on the southern skyline.

The tallest is the Jim Pattison Pavilion of Vancouver General Hospital (VGH). Established in 1886 by the Canadian Pacific Railway, VGH began as a nine-bed tent hospital. Today the institution has evolved into the largest tertiary/quaternary research academic medical centre in British Columbia.

The 17-storey, 55,832-m^2 tower, completed in May 2003, is named after local billionaire Jimmy Pattison, who made a $20 million contribution to prostate research at VGH. The top floor, with its spectacular views of the North Shore, is the palliative care unit—a compassionate gesture on the part of hospital planners and administrators.

To the east of VGH is a 14-storey building with round windows, the new home of the BC Cancer Research Centre. It was designed by the IBI Group/Henriquez Partners and opened in 2004. Some 60 principal scientists and 600 technical and medical staff work there, including the Genome Sciences Centre staff who sequenced the SARS virus. Both the interior and exterior design of this building reflects the work of the researchers and responds to our own fascination with DNA and its impact on all aspects of our lives. The top-floor meeting room has an amoeba-shaped roof. An outside stairway resembling the DNA double helix connects the office tower to the lab building. The 68 round windows front and back have coloured glass strips representing chromosome 8. The window shape is that of Petri dishes used for scientific experiments—a creative

Guide continues on p. 29

tion to the large sandbar that one day would become Granville Island. Dionisio Galiano, who was in the area at the same time, also did not find, or chose to ignore, the Creek area. It wasn't until 1859 that Captain George Richards of the Royal Navy made the first maps of the Creek.

By 1867 the early settlers had begun to realize the potential of the vast forests surrounding them. The main industry in the Creek area became forestry related, with Captain Stamp and Captain Moody developing mills and beginning to ship lumber to international destinations. Land owned by Stamp's Mill (later named Hastings Mill on Burrard Inlet) made up 43 per cent of the area of present-day Vancouver.

Geologically, False Creek is part of the trough from New Westminster and the North Fraser River that includes Burnaby Lake and may have once been a northerly channel of the Fraser River. This trough aided the building of a flume from Trout Lake, located southeast of the creek, to float logs to the sawmills at Hastings Mill on Burrard Inlet.

Granville Island was originally a sandbar of more than 20 acres surrounded by water. The Squamish people had used the Creek area for centuries as a fishing site and winter camping area. The sandbar made a perfect location to build fishing weirs at low tide and to guide in trout, sturgeon, flounder and smelt for an easier catch as the tides came in. (The Sandbar Restaurant located on the Island gets its name from this early geography of the area.)

The present Granville Island was Crown land that was reclaimed in 1916 when 36 acres was created by Harbour Commission dredging operations that piled fill within wooden walls. The Harbour Commission paid $1 to Ottawa to gain title to the sandbar and held control for nearly 60 years until the Canada Mortgage and Hous-

History continues on p. 30

touch that chief architect Henriquez claims for himself.

The building to the far east with the flag is City Hall. Unlike now, when it opened in 1936 it was far from the downtown centre of business and commerce. Today, the mayor and councillors make sure citizens know where the municipal decisions are made.

All these landmarks, and all the buildings on the slopes south of False Creek, are in an area long called Fairview Slopes. In the early years of Vancouver this area did not have a "fair view," but one of grime, smoke, pollution and filth. Looking beyond, there was—and still is—the spectacular view of the North Shore mountains, now somewhat obscured by towering condos. It was in Fairview in 1915 that the University of British Columbia was originally situated, in several huts.

The present street layout and street names in Fairview were set out in 1887 before clearing and housing construction began in 1889. Streets were named by the CPR land commissioner, L.A. Hamilton, who had a liking for tree names such as Alder, Arbutus, Birch etc., presumably intending them to be in alphabetical order. Reports have it that when Hamilton left town the draftsman who completed the street maps didn't have a similarly orderly mind, and so the streets now progress in a haphazard sequence of Larch, Balsam, Vine, Yew, Arbutus, Maple and so on.

Leg in Boot Square, slightly west of the waterfront restaurant Monk McQueen's, was so named because in the late 1800s, a human leg, complete with boot, was washed up on the industrial shoreline. Police put the leg up in the square, hoping someone would identify it, but no one-legged (or two-legged) person claimed it.

After passing under the Cambie Street bridge, look across an empty lot to the red Domtar Salt Building, a facility built in 1931 that was used to store and distribute salt. With any luck it will be saved as a heritage building. In a 1997 planning report for the area that was then labelled Creekside Landing, it was suggested that the building be moved to the proposed southeast False Creek Village Square to join a commercial cluster to be located there. All of these former

Guide continues on p. 31

A great blue heron surveys False Creek.

False Creek shacks, ca. 1934. Photo courtesy City of Vancouver Archives.

ing Corporation took it over in 1973. The cost to create the Island was $342,000 in 1916 dollars.

By 1923 all of Granville Island's industrial lots were occupied with factories for rope, boilers, barrels, chains, drums, roofing, coal, building supplies, cement, paint, steel rivets and band saws. Because of the heavy industrial nature of the Island it was briefly called Industrial Island.

From 1920 to 1930 there was some attempt to clean up the shores and east mud flats, which were converted into False Creek Park (now Strathcona Park). Squatters continued to live in houseboats and shacks along the shores. General decay in the industrial plants set in during the Depression and fires occurred in the sawmills.

The Second World War years benefited the Creek with an increase in shipbuilding. After the war, propos-

History continues on p. 32

plans to have a "sustainable community" within this area may now be changed, since the southeast side of the Creek is to be developed for the athletes village during the 2010 Winter Olympics.

At the end of the Creek, the large, silver bubble you see was long known as Science World. In 2004, Telus Corporation, a communications provider, agreed to contribute $9 million over 15 years to sponsor the facility and its programs. In exchange, the building's name was changed to TELUSphere. The building was one of the Canadian exhibition buildings for Expo 86. During construction workers had to use rock climbing gear to do the caulking of the exterior panels. Inside are numerous interactive science and technology exhibits and one of the world's largest domed movie screens, towering more than five storeys high.

Looking northwest from the eastern end of False Creek to the mountains, you will see The Lions—two large, conical rocks in the North Shore Mountains with a height of 1525 m. There is a legend that the peaks represent the twin daughters of a chief who warred with the northern tribes. When the twins came of age the enemies were invited to come and celebrate. They brought gifts of peace, and therefore the twins, for their role as early peacekeepers, were given immortality and placed in a high spot. Miners are said to have irreverently called the mountains "Sheba's Paps."

From this perspective you can also see the ornate green cupola roof of the Sun Tower. The home of the Vancou-

Guide continues on p. 33

TELUSphere, with the Skytrain running by

False Creek from Granville Island to TELUS*phere – 31*

Granville Island as "Industrial Island," ca. 1931. Photo by W.G. Moore, courtesy City of Vancouver Archives.

als about what to do with the increasingly filthy Creek area began to emerge. Some suggestions were made for continued use of the Creek for its industrial value, or to completely fill it in to increase the amount of industrial land available. Costs were prohibitive for filling in the entire expanse. The tracts at the east end had been filled in during construction of the railway terminals during the early 1900s. Additional fill-ins were the small portion under Granville Bridge to link Granville Island to the mainland and, in 1964, the area near Main Street.

Numerous fires on Granville Island and general rot in the buildings meant many tenants left for better quarters during the 1950s and '60s. The last sawmill in

History continues on p. 34

ver Sun newspaper from 1924–1964, it held the record of "tallest building in the British Empire" when it was completed in 1912. At 82 m, it was also the tallest building in Canada for two years until Toronto beat us out with the 20-storey Royal Bank building.

In 1872, just beyond the TELUSphere, the first bridge was built over the False Creek mudflats. The present site of Main Street, it gave access from New Westminster to the growing settlement of Granville (now the Gastown area). It was in this southeast location of the Creek that the area's first industrial plant, a slaughterhouse, was developed. By 1918 the tidal flats that extended well into the Strathcona area of the city were filled in and became the site of the CNR and Great Northern Railway stations, freight sheds and rail yards.

In 1986, Expo 86 was held on 56.6 hectares of the north shore of the Creek, stretching from Quebec Street to the Yaletown area. It had the theme of transportation and was the largest special-category World Exposition held in North America. The Skytrain that you see zooming to and from downtown was launched in 1985 as Vancouver's own example of efficient transportation.

After Expo 86 the land was purchased by Concord Pacific, owned by billionaire Li Ka Shing, for $320 million over 15 years, with the agreement that Li would build condos and mixed-use condominium developments on the property. When the $3 billion project is completed, it will double the population of the downtown core and once again completely redesign

Guide continues on p. 35

Sun Tower, with The Lions in the distance

False Creek from Granville Island to TELUSphere – 33

the Creek area was that of B.C. Forest Products, which burned down in 1960.

In 1967 a land exchange between the CPR, the provincial government and the City of Vancouver resulted in the city being the major holder of land along the Creek. The following year saw city council lift the industrial designation, which made possible the dramatic developments in the entire Creek area.

Disputes continued between city council, consultants and university students over whether False Creek should continue to be primarily industrial or include housing, parks and recreation areas. Finally in 1973, under the guidance of the Minister for Urban Affairs, the Island was taken over by the Canada Mortgage and Housing Corporation, eventually to become the most financially successful renewal project ever sponsored by Ottawa. Of the more than $25 million budgeted for the project, $5.5 million was returned to the Treasury Board when the form and function of the present Granville Island emerged for less cost than expected!

In July 1979 Granville Island opened for business as an urban market, a home for light industry and businesses, and a favourite Vancouver destination.

ભ્

the shoreline of False Creek. By 2010 at least 15,000 additional people are expected to move here, where the average one-bedroom condominium unit costs over $200,000.

Progressing along the northwest shore of False Creek, you will see the large, white dome of BC Place Stadium. It was built in the early '80s at a cost of $100 million. The stadium was the first covered stadium in Canada and was the largest air-supported dome by area (40,468 m²) in the world. The roof is made of two layers of fibreglass woven fabric covered with Teflon. The two layers of fabric have four feet of space between them. It is used by the BC Lions football team and for tradeshows and concerts. In any given year, over 200 events are staged within its climate-controlled environment. Depending on the outside temperature, it costs at least $500 an hour to heat the over 2 million m³ (83.5 million ft³) of air that is pumped inside and keeps the roof up. On the rare occasions when snow covers the dome, hot air can be pumped in between the layers to melt snow on the roof.

Other buildings in this area include General Motors Place and the Plaza of Nations. GM Place, or "The Garage" as it is known by locals, was built in 1995 to house the city's NHL hockey and NBA basketball franchises, rock concerts and hundreds of other events in state-of-the-art facilities. The Plaza

Granville Island today

False Creek from Granville Island to TELUSphere – 35

Paddling False Creek past Brush with Illumination

of Nations is another relic of Expo 86, now housing a variety of offices, night clubs, a casino and a glass-covered stage notorious for its bad sound. Portions of the demonstration monorail track from Expo can still be seen running under the glass roof.

If you look at the northwest skyline you will see the Sheraton Wall building. At 137 m and 48 storeys, it is the tallest building in the city. The developer, a Mr. Wall, had chosen a dark silver-blue for the window colour, but when the structure was half built the city insisted he had agreed to a lighter glass colour. The city sued and Wall countersued. The compromise was that the bottom 30 storeys, housing a hotel, were completed with dark glass and the top 18 (containing 74 luxury condos selling from $575,000 to $4 million) were completed with lighter glass. Wall got the last word, though, by buying dark blinds and using reflective glass so that the windows still look dark in the sunshine. There is an annual event called "Climb the Wall" where participants climb up the stairwells of the building to raise money to combat lung disease.

In 2005, the Wall building was superseded in height by a 60-storey commercial/residential tower in the downtown core which will contain a luxury, five-star Shangri-La Hotel occupying the lower 15 floors. Floors 16 to 42 will have 227 homes ranging in price from $400,000 to $1.4 million, while floors 43 to 60 will have 66 private-access estates with 360-degree views of the mountains, city, Stanley Park and English Bay. Yours for a mere $1.6 million to $5.5 million.

The pointed, green, copper-clad roof of the Hotel Vancouver peeks from among the towering office buildings that surround it. It is the third hotel of this name to be built in the same general area. The first was a wooden building that was more like an inn or farmhouse. In 1916, Vancouver society flocked to the newest Hotel Vancouver as the place to see and be seen at the social events of the burgeoning city. Construction of the present hotel began in the late 1920s, financed by the Canadian National Railway. Completion was delayed by the Great Depression, and it took 11 years and a joint financing of $12 million by both Canadian National and Canadian Pacific to finish the project in 1939.

Looking back at seawall level, under and east of the Cambie Street Bridge, you will pass by Coopers Park, where the Sweeney sawmill and cooperage were situated from 1921 to 1982. Sweeney's had become one of the largest barrel makers in the British Commonwealth before it was demolished to make way for Expo 86. The first Cambie Street Bridge was built in 1891 to provide access to a sawmill on the south shore. In 1911 a metal bridge with a swinging centre span was built and named the Connaught Bridge

A solo paddler tries to keep up with the team.

after the Duchess of Connaught, who opened it. In 1984, it was replaced by the present bridge, built by the same company that went on to build the Confederation Bridge from New Brunswick to Prince Edward Island.

Starting in Coopers Park and for part of the way back to Granville Island, you will encounter a variety of public art installations. Commissioned by Concord Pacific to meet a condition of its land purchase, these works often draw on elements of the area's past or natural history for inspiration.

At Quayside Marina you can see suspended silhouettes of archival pictures depicting early Vancouver and at sidewalk level, stone walls with some of the history of the Creek area chiselled into them. This project, made in 1996 by Bernie Miller and Alan Tregabov, is called *Street Light*.

Look along the curving fence that follows the seawall to see *Welcome to the Land of Light* by Henry Tsang. The sentences are printed in English and Chinook, which was a jargon developed in the 19th century with First Nations to use as a trade language. To save you trying to read these words, which will appear backwards to water-borne art lovers, the phrases say

GREETING GOOD YOU ARRIVE
HERE WHERE LIGHT BE UNDER,
LAND FUTURE IT BE NOW, HERE
YOU BEGIN LIVE LIKE NEW,
WHERE PEOPLE TALK DIFFER-

Marking High Tide: *"The moon circles the earth and the ocean responds with the rhythm of the tides."*

ENT BUT GOOD TOGETHER, IF YOUR HEART MIND OPEN YOU RECEIVE NEW KNOWLEDGE, YOU HAVE SAME LIKE ELECTRIC EYE AND HEART MIND AND TALK SOUND, YOU LIVE FAST LIKE LIGHT, SEE TALK BE HERE THERE AND EVERYWHERE AT ONE TIME, US MAKE THIS COMMUNITY GOOD INDEED, YOU NOT AFRAID HERE, HERE YOU BEGIN, LIVE LIKE CHIEF, WORLD SAME LIKE IN YOUR HAND.

In the next bay you will find *Brush with Illumination*. One of the Creek's most obvious pieces of public art, it was created in 1998 by Buster Simpson. The brush depicts an ancient writing tool—the calligraphy brush. It is suspended over what is described on the artist's website as the "inkwell" of False Creek. The solar panels aid in collecting environmental information, which is transmitted and translated into ideograms (symbols that stand for the object itself). A sign warns boaters of its sudden movements as the base of the brush floats on the tides. To fully appreciate this modern, interactive work of art, visit the creator's website at www.brush-delux.com.

The circle of granite boulders at the east end of the bay, called *Waiting for Low Tide*, is echoed a bit farther to the west in a massive concrete ring resting horizontally on pillars, called *Marking High Tide*. An inscription on the inside of the concrete circle reads "The moon circles the earth and the ocean responds with the rhythm of the tides." These artworks, designed by landscape architect Don Vaughan,

Cormorants enjoying a Brush with Illumination

encourage the viewer to visualize the dramatic tidal changes in the Creek and appreciate the beauty of the stones, which were found on the north False Creek site and given significance by their placement here.

A new installation called *Khenko the Fisher*, by Doug Taylor, is planned for the northwest side of the bay in 2005–2006. It will be made of tubular aluminum and will move with the wind. "Khenko" is the First Nations name for the blue heron. Before the Creek got polluted by industrialization, there were at least 57 salmon streams entering it, which provided an abundance of fish for herons. Taylor's movable art will celebrate the return of the heron to False Creek as the water once again becomes clean. Great blue herons are over a metre tall, with a wing span of nearly two metres and have ancient origins dating back more than 57 million years. Herons live in the Fraser River estuary and in Stanley Park, so when you see them flying home in the evening, they are heading for one of these two spots and their rooms with a view.

The green *Glass Umbrellas*, also designed by Don Vaughan, shine at night like a beacon or lighthouse and can be a rain shelter at any time of the day or night. They define the promontory at the side of David Lam Park (named for the first Chinese Lieutenant Governor of British Columbia).

Yaletown, the area to the north between the Cambie and Granville bridges and bordered by Richards Street on the northwest, is now a tourist destination and upscale residential area. The old brick buildings, now gloriously renovated, are some of the last vestiges of the industrial history of the north side of the Creek. Yaletown got its name when the CPR moved its construction equipment and repair shops from Yale in the Fraser Canyon to Vancouver. The district was populated by industrial and railway workers, usually single men and was probably every Vancouver mother's nightmare. The Yaletown "bachelor boys" lived downtown and in the previously mentioned floating shacks, and no doubt enjoyed wine, women and song. Hmmm—perhaps not that different from Yaletown boys today, except that the quality of the real estate has improved.

Paddling past the Yaletown shacks of today

In 1885 the Canadian Pacific Railway moved its western terminus from Port Moody to Vancouver. In exchange for this extension of the rail line, the company obtained 2,430 hectares of land, including the downtown core and extending south to the Fraser River. The next CPR plan was for a terminus at Kitsilano Point, with a proposal for a deep ocean port including numerous docks. Offered another exchange, this time of a 20-year tax exemption for the Yaletown area, the company decided to build its terminus, including train yard shops and a roundhouse, on the north shore of the Creek instead. Despite having accepted that deal, however, the CPR nevertheless continued to plan for wharves and other port installations on Kitsilano Point. To make their point (so to speak), they maintained a rail bridge across to the Point from downtown from 1886 to 1982. This bridge also was part of the early interurban passenger rail system that extended to Marpole on the North Fraser River. Although the bridge was removed in 1982, the CPR still owns the rail line, and the Arbutus rail line extension continues to provoke animated discussion over its future use. The CPR, following its long tradition of profiting from both transportation and real estate, continues to propose development of a narrow corridor of apartments, condominiums and townhouses on the track property, while the city of Vancouver and most of the residents in the area urge that the Arbutus extension be used as a rails-to-trails bicycle route or a historical streetcar line or some other type of low-key transportation corridor.

The Roundhouse in Yaletown has been converted from its original use of changing the direction of locomotives, into a community centre. The only remaining railway equipment is Engine #374, which pulled the first train from Montreal to Vancouver, in May 1887.

When extensive logging occurred on the south shore, Granville Street was the main route for skidding logs down to the Creek. As an extension of the street, the first Granville Bridge was built in 1889, followed by a metal drawbridge in 1909. Streetcars stopped on Granville Bridge and there were steps down to the Island so workers could get to the "Industrial Island." The present eight-lane bridge was completed in 1953. All the bridges used the Granville Island sandbar for part of their footings.

Now, although the trip has come to an end, the best part of it may be when you—competent, athletic, urban kayaker that you are—paddle by and wave to all those envious, land-bound tourists on the Granville Market decks, on your way back to your launch site.

*There is nothing
—absolutely nothing
—half so much worth doing
as simply messing about in boats.*

—from Wind in the Willows,
by Kenneth Grahame (1859–1932)

2 English Bay from False Creek to Siwash Rock

Difficulty Beginner conditions – low risk

Distance 3.5 nmi round trip

Duration 1.5–2.5 hours round trip

Charts
3311 Sunshine Coast—Vancouver Harbour to Desolation Sound, 1:40,000
3481 Approaches to Vancouver Harbour, 1:25,000
3493 Vancouver Harbour, Western Portion, 1:10,000

Launching and take-out sites

The easiest place to launch is next to the Kitsilano Point Coast Guard station in Vanier Park. There is a boat ramp and small sand beach. In front of the Maritime Museum there is also a small beach with a sheltered launch site. This is a popular place for people to practise rescue techniques and rolling in the summer. You can launch from two places on Granville Island: the Ecomarine Ocean Kayak Centre dock and a small dock in Alder Bay near the False Creek Community Centre. If you plan on using the Ecomarine dock, it is a good idea to ask the staff in the store so you do not interfere with their rental operation, especially on weekends in the summer.

Getting there

Access to this route is not difficult, but may require a good map of the city if you are unfamiliar with the area. Kitsilano Point Coast Guard station, Vanier Park and the Maritime Museum can be accessed from Chestnut Street, north of Cornwall Street at the western base of the Burrard Street Bridge. Continue straight north for the Maritime Museum, or, for the Coast Guard station and Vanier Park, turn east on Whyte Avenue, passing by the Planetarium and the Royal Conservatory of Music.

Granville Island is best accessed from 4th Avenue. Heading east, follow the signs directing you to turn north, immediately passing under the main span of the Granville Street Bridge onto Anderson Street. If heading west, you will turn onto Anderson Street just before the main span of the bridge. There is a large billboard, often advertising the Public Market, on your right as a landmark. The roads on the Island are all one way, so proceed with caution if you are unfamiliar with the area.

Parking

As with the False Creek trip, pay parking is the order of the day. Pay parking is available in the large lot closest to the water by the Coast Guard station, but if you are lucky you may find an empty free spot across from the Vancouver Archives or in front of the Vancouver Museum. There is pay parking in front of the Maritime Museum. Be careful about parking on the street in the Kitsilano Point area if you are launching from the Maritime

Museum, as it is mostly permit parking only.

While there are hundreds of free parking spots on Granville Island, you'll need patience to secure one. It is not as bad as it seems, with spots opening up all the time. Just obey the signs. Parking for even a few minutes over the posted time (generally three hours) will result in a ticket. This can be avoided if you park in one of the pay lots or move your vehicle "off Island."

Washrooms

Ecomarine Ocean Kayak Centre, Granville Island Public Market (open 8:00 am to 6:00 pm only), Vancouver Parks Board washrooms to the east of the Coast Guard station, the Bathhouse at English Bay Beach, and Vancouver Parks Board concessions at Second and Third Beaches.

Paddling considerations

English Bay is an amazing place to paddle, in large part because of the diversity of conditions you will encounter, from picture perfect, glassy smooth water, to six-foot waves breaking over the seawall. While this makes for exciting paddling at times, paddlers must be adequately prepared for the conditions, as there are no protected pull-outs other than the small bay near the Maritime Museum. On hot days in the summer the wind generally builds throughout the day, with strong winds blowing from the west most afternoons. In the summer the channel under Burrard Bridge

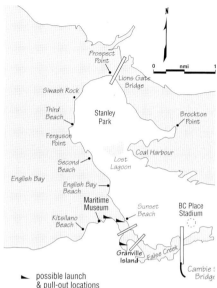

➤ possible launch & pull-out locations

becomes congested with a constant stream of pleasure boats and is best avoided. The coast along Stanley Park between English Bay Beach and Siwash Rock is a shallow shoal. Watch for exposed rocks at lower tides.

The route

As you leave False Creek or if departing from Vanier Park, to the east you will see Burrard Bridge. This bridge opened in 1932 and is the most ornate of any of the seven bridges linking Vancouver to other municipalities or across False Creek. This decorative design is a result of advice given by an urban planner who was asked to give guidance on how to improve what was still a rough and ready seaport. He is said to have replied, "Build beautiful bridges." The coat

Paddling in English Bay, the West End in the background

of arms is an early one for the City of Vancouver—"By sea and land we prosper"—and decorates the towers along with lion heads and figureheads on boat bows. Inside the towers there are no ghosts, no secret treasures or condominium housing. Initially the north arch held the electrical wiring for the bridge lights.

Staff of the Kitsilano Coast Guard station on the south shore provide 24-hour service to boaters, commercial marine traffic and even kayakers in Howe Sound, South Georgia Strait, English Bay, False Creek, Vancouver Harbour and Indian Arm. While the present building is only about 10 years old, the station has been in the Kitsilano location since 1964. The Coast Guard responds to an average of 235 life-threatening events a year,

such as search and rescue for divers or boats adrift. They also deal with oil spills in False Creek, repair of navigational aids such as the lights on the buoys at the entry of False Creek, and matters such as traffic control and illegal anchoring. The Coast Guard members from this station are often the first responders to marine fires in the Creek. Because they are used to dealing with marine fires, they know to use foam instead of water (an important difference if you don't want the boat in question to sink!).

The Kitsilano Coast Guard station has a 41-foot search and rescue boat, the *Osprey*, and a Hurricane fast-response craft, *Osprey 1*, capable of speeds up to 45 knots.

The Kitsilano Coast Guard staff remind all kayakers that they must wear a PFD (personal flotation device). It is the law. As well, kayaks, like all waterborne vessels, must follow the marine rules of the road. Give way to commercial traffic, stay as far to the right of the channels in and out of False Creek as possible, and do not interfere with transit of tow boats. A scary reminder given by the Coast Guard: if you think it might be fun to race a moving deep-sea ship, don't! If you get any closer than half a kilometre, the ship's crew cannot see you under the slant of their bow.

In 1928 when False Creek was surrounded by industries, floating homes and shanties, the first fire boat, the *J.H. Carlisle*, was commissioned by the owners of industries on the Creek for their exclusive use. It was used for 40 years on the Creek. There are now two fire boats run by the Vancouver Fire Department and available to False Creek waterfront homes or boaters in the event of an emergency.

Vanier Park, on the south shore, is named after the Canadian Governor General Georges Vanier. It was the site of the Kitsilano Indian reserve until 1913, when 29 hectares was purchased for $218,750. In 2002, the British Columbia Court of Appeal ruled that a small, four-hectare area under the Burrard Street Bridge and next to the Molson Brewery was to be returned to the Squamish people.

Vanier Park hosts a number of festivals: the Children's Festival (May), Bard on the Beach (June to September) and an annual Kite Festival.

The Vancouver Museum, located in Vanier Park, was founded in 1894 as the Art, Historical and Scientific Association of Vancouver. The museum moved to its present building in 1968. It is Canada's largest civic museum, exhibiting both permanent and travelling exhibits. The H.R. MacMillan

Landing by the Maritime Museum

English Bay from False Creek to Siwash Rock – 45

Planetarium, attached to the museum, has star and laser light and music shows in the evenings. The conical shape of its roof represents the shape of the woven, cedar-bark hats of the Haida First Nations people. On clear nights and for special celestial events, the Pacific Space Centre, the little domed building beside the museum, opens up its observatory for viewing the night sky.

The Maritime Museum, with its tall, triangular shape, houses the *St. Roch*, a wooden icebreaker famous for being the first vessel to traverse the Northwest Passage from west to east (1940–42) and the first to do it from east to west in a single season (1944).

When it sailed to Halifax via the Panama Canal in 1950 and returned to Vancouver in 1954, it became the first ship to have circumnavigated North America in both directions.

The large, yellow and white, cigar-shaped object in front of the Maritime Museum is the *Ben Franklin* submersible. Volunteers have restored the exterior and will complete the inside as funding allows. The 48-foot submersible played a major role in the investigation of the Gulf Stream drift in 1969 when six crew drifted for 30 days from Palm Beach, Florida, to just south of Halifax, Nova Scotia. Additional objectives of the voyage were to investigate the effects on crews of

Historic ships can still be found at the Maritime Museum dock.

living for long periods in a totally closed environment, analogous to space travel, and to explore and demonstrate the engineering capabilities of a submersible vehicle.

Visible behind the *St. Roch* and the Maritime Museum is a 30-metre totem pole. It was carved by Chief Mungo Martin of the Kwakiutl nation for British Columbia's centenary celebrations in 1958 and is a replica of one given to Queen Elizabeth II.

Go into the little cove in front of the Maritime Museum and see the boats at the Historic Boat Dock. The *Sea Lion*, built in 1905, was the only B.C. tug to have a piano in its saloon, and the first one to get ship-to-shore radio, in 1922. Its whistle runs seven notes up and six notes down. The tug towed spruce logs from the Queen Charlottes to mills on the mainland to make airplanes during the First World War.

Now head carefully across the mouth of the creek to the north shore, where, when you look back to the east, you will see a dark brown, windowless structure. This is the Vancouver Aquatic Centre, the city's busiest public pool, with over 250,000 annual visits. Opened in 1974, the centre houses a 50-metre pool, a dive tank with a 10-metre platform, and a fitness facility.

Heading west, you enter English Bay—named by the English Captain Vancouver, who came to the area in 1792—and look out toward the Strait of Georgia. On your right is Sunset Beach, a well-loved viewpoint for enjoying beautiful B.C. sunsets and great views of the summer fireworks in English Bay. It is also the destination for annual peace marches that, at their peak, saw tens of thousands of demonstrators cross the Burrard Bridge from Kitsilano to rally here.

Past Sunset Beach, on a small peninsula, you will see a large human-like stone figure. *The Inukshuk* was originally constructed by Alvin Kanak of Rankin Inlet for the Northwest Territories pavilion at Expo 86. In the flat, barren lands of the Arctic, the Inuit build inukshuks to mark paths to the best hunting grounds. Inukshuks also indicated where food was stored or warned of dangerous places. The Inuit would stuff arctic heather into openings in an inukshuk so that when the boughs waved in the wind they would scare the caribou toward the hunters.

Inukshuk on north shore of English Bay

Look for a unique, sky-high tree as you pass English Bay Beach.

Further along is English Bay Beach, which has been a popular summertime destination ever since sand was added in 1898. It may be hard to imagine now, but in the early days, sun worshippers had to bushwhack through forest to reach the beach, and upon arrival they would discover a beach divided into a men's side and a women's side by a large rock in the centre. In the early 1900s a wooden bathhouse and a long wooden pier featuring a glassed-in dance hall called "The Prom" were built. The existing concrete building, with its arched doors, is a bathhouse built in 1931. The annual New Year's Day Polar Bear Swim, first started by Peter Pantages and nine crazy friends in 1920, now sees up to 2,000 brave or insane swimmers kick off the New Year, and maybe a hangover, with a quick dip in frigid English Bay waters.

The landmark Sylvia Hotel, built in 1912 as an apartment block, is often barely visible behind its façade of Virginia creeper. At the time of its construction it was the West End's tallest and grandest building. Just to the west of the Sylvia, if you look way up, you will see a tall pin oak tree atop an apartment building. The tree has its own large funnel of dirt, a small lawn about its roots, and an automatic watering system. A pin oak often keeps its brown leaves until the new ones bud in the spring and gets its name from the pins, or building pegs, that could be made from its wood because of its extraordinarily straight grain. Amazingly, this tree was placed here to represent the height of the first growth Douglas firs that used to exist in the area. These coniferous trees would often be 76 to 122 metres (25 to 40 storeys) tall.

The south entrance to Stanley Park follows and then Second Beach. The salt water swimming pool, which provides fun for children and adults alike, is a recent replacement for the original "draw and fill" pool that used high tide to replace the pool water with fresh sea water. Both Second and Third Beach had sand and fill imported to provide the beach area. Second beach was at one time also a campground for thousands of miners on their way from Victoria to the gold mines of the Fraser River in 1858.

Stanley Park was originally named "Coal Peninsula" after coal was discovered on the shores of Burrard Inlet.

Not enough coal was ever found there to be commercially viable, but we still ended up with a Coal Harbour on the Vancouver harbour side of the park.

In the late 1850s, Stanley Park was a military reserve maintained to defend the area from the possibility of a U.S. invasion. Logging operations meant that much of the old growth cedar, pine, hemlock and Douglas fir, especially in the area of Brockton Point, were cut down. The present forest is mainly second or third growth trees.

When the City of Vancouver was incorporated in 1886, the first thing the new council did was to persuade the federal government to retain the

James Cunningham supervising seawall construction, 1963. Photo courtesy City of Vancouver Archives.

English Bay from False Creek to Siwash Rock – 49

peninsula for a park. It has also been suggested that a few landowners put pressure on council to keep the land as a park because they were worried that making more real estate available in the West End would devalue their properties. The park was officially opened in 1889 and named after Sir Frederic Arthur Stanley, who was Governor General of Canada at the time. Encompassing 404.7 hectares, it is Canada's largest city-funded park.

The Stanley Park Seawall extends nearly 9 km around the circumference of Stanley Park. Construction of the present wall began near Second Beach in 1917. Crafty local politicians were able to get federal funding to extend the wall around the park,

by pointing out the need to stop the erosion caused by the wake of ships passing through the First Narrows to the ports in Burrard Inlet, and by storms on the English Bay side. Since the park was on a 99-year lease from Ottawa, the feds agreed to protect their property. For 32 years, stonemason James Cunningham laboured to complete the seawall. Even after he retired he would return to "supervise" the work. After he died in 1963, it took another 17 years to finish the remaining 2.5 km of wall. The completed seawall officially opened in 1980. Cunningham's ashes are in the wall near Siwash Rock, and an annual run around the seawall is held in his honour. Today the Vancouver seawall

Balancing stones: "an experience of transience"

is one of the city's major attractions, running uninterrupted for 23 km from CRAB Park near Canada Place to Kitsilano Point Park.

The building at Ferguson Point was an officers mess and observation post during the Second World War, when Stanley Park once again became a military post to protect the Vancouver harbour. Later it became the Teahouse Restaurant and was recently renamed Sequoia Grill for the sequoia trees that grow in the area.

Close to Ferguson Point, and depending on whether the tide is in or out, and on the whim of their builder, you may see a series of "balancing stones." Kent Avery builds these structures without glue and each day reconstructs new ones after the tides knock them down. Avery says he does this because it is "an experience of transience."

North of the Third Beach concession, above the seawall, is the largest red alder tree in Canada—30 m tall and 1.8 m wide. Close to Third Beach, at Ferguson Point, there is a memorial to Pauline Johnson, a famous Canadian poet who wrote such poems as "The Song My Paddle Sings." From 1941 to 1945 there were gun emplacements and munitions stores at Third Beach.

The 10-metre-high, freestanding pillar of rock you will soon see is known as Siwash Rock.

The Legend of Siwash Rock tells of how a young Indian warrior was turned to stone by four supernatural giants when he refused to move because he was cleansing himself in preparation for the birth of his first child. The supernatural beings were at first unsure how to deal with someone disobeying them, but eventually decided that the warrior should stand forever as a monument to pure fatherhood. Two smaller rocks are in the hills above Siwash Rock and are said to represent the wife and child.

During the First World War there was an artillery battery above Siwash Rock. Once, a Stanley Park goat escaped the zoo and somehow managed to spend some time up on top of the rock.

Some things never change: Siwash Rock, 1908. Photo courtesy Vancouver Public Library.

Kitsilano Beach with bathhouse and dance hall. Photo courtesy Vancouver Public Library.

Looking north you will see three modest mountains: Hollyburn Mountain in Cypress Provincial Park, Grouse Mountain and Mount Seymour.

The ski hills on Grouse have vertical drops of 365 metres. Snowboarding and downhill freestyle will be held on these hills during the 2010 Olympics. The Grouse Grind (parallel to the gondola route) was built from 1981–83 by two mountaineers to climb up the hill for exercise. These days, racers can do it in 28 minutes, while a walking pace is 1 hour 20 minutes. The gondola takes about five minutes up or down.

Mount Seymour is named after the second Governor of British Columbia. He had opposed Confederation, but British Columbia joined Canada anyway in 1871, a decision aided by the federal lure of payment of the provincial debt.

Turn back now. Kayaking under the Lions Gate Bridge and in the Vancouver Harbour is not permitted.

Returning the way you came, you will see Kitsilano Beach and Kitsilano Point on the south as you enter the mouth of False Creek. This area was the winter fishing village of Snauq, home of Squamish First Nation people. Kitsilano Beach was named after Chief Khahtsahlano (Haatsa-Lah-Nogh), the Squamish chief whose tribe once owned the area before the Canadian Pacific Railway expropriated the land in 1886. During the Second World War, Kitsilano Beach was used for practising commando raids and beach assaults. Luckily, this use has long since changed to daily summertime assaults by hordes of scantily clad beachgoers and volleyball players.

In 1914–15, a proposal was put forward by Swan, a city engineer, to use plans of the Chicago, Milwaukee, St. Paul & Pacific Railway company and develop Kitsilano Point into a deep-sea shipping port complete with multiple wharfs, tall industrial buildings and company housing. This mega-development plan makes the present million-dollar housing, park, beach and even the new, hotly contested restaurant being built on Kitsilano Beach look pretty acceptable by comparison.

Now back to your launch site and views from land of the present-day city and Stanley Park.

And up on the hills against the sky,
A fir tree rocking its lullaby,
Swings, swings,
Its emerald wings,
Swelling the song that my paddle sings.

from The Song My Paddle Sings,
by E. Pauline Johnson
(Tekahionwake) (1861–1913),
who is buried near Siwash Rock

Tents along Kitsilano Beach, 1904. Photo courtesy Vancouver Public Library.

3 English Bay from Jericho to Wreck Beach and Log Booms

Difficulty Beginner conditions – low risk

Distance 8 nmi round trip

Duration 3.5 hours round trip

Charts 3311 Sunshine Coast—Vancouver Harbour to Desolation Sound,1:40,000
3481 Approaches to Vancouver Harbour, 1:25,000
3491 Fraser River, North Arm, 1:20,000
3493 Vancouver Harbour, Western Portion, 1:10,000

Launching and take-out sites

The easiest place to launch is immediately to the east of the Jericho Sailing Centre compound. Park at the end of the parking lot and carry your boats about 150 m to protected waters behind the Jericho Beach Pier. You need to be a member of Jericho sailing club to use their dollies and boat ramps.

Alternatively you can park and launch from any one of the parking lots along Spanish Banks to the west of the Jericho Sailing Centre.

Getting there

Head west on 4th Avenue in Vancouver. Two blocks after Alma Street you will see the large Jericho Beach Park on your right. About 700 m further along, the road will split, with 4th Avenue continuing up the hill to the left. Take the right exit onto Northwest Marine Drive. Follow Marine Drive as it curves downhill for about 300 m, then turn right onto Discovery Street. This runs directly into the sailing centre. At the end of the road, turn in to the parking lot on your right. Park at the extreme east end for the easiest access to the water.

Parking

The parking lot in front of the sailing centre is pay parking only from May until September. If you want to avoid paying you can drop off your boats and then park your car in one of the many free parking lots a little further west on Marine Drive.

Washrooms

The Jericho Sailing Centre has the only washrooms in the immediate area. Go upstairs in the big white hangar building. Vancouver Parks Board washrooms are available at Jericho, Locarno and Spanish Banks concessions.

Paddling considerations

There is nudity on Wreck Beach (not that there is anything wrong with that).

If you go around Point Grey into the Strait of Georgia in the direction of the log booms, be aware of working tugs. At low tides, the Spanish Banks area becomes a large, wet sandbar, which may require you to paddle far from the shoreline and add considerable distance to your trip. Large sailing boats frequently have races out from Royal Vancouver Yacht Club.

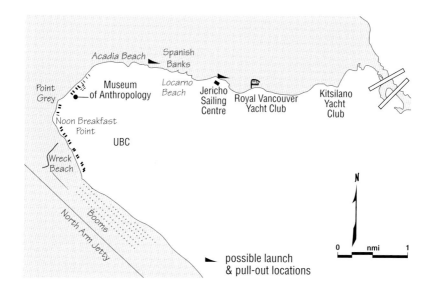

possible launch
& pull-out locations

Large standing waves can be found at the mouth of the Fraser near the log booms when an incoming tide meets the fast flowing river.

The route

Paddling in the Point Grey area requires us to look a little further back in history than in other areas. Findings from a coastal site on Pender Island in the Gulf Islands indicated that the culture of the aboriginal people was well established in the Pacific Northwest more than 3,500 years ago. Archaeologists have established that there has been habitation at Jericho Beach for more than 3,000 years. A First Nations Musqueam site called Eyalmu—"good spring water"—was located close to here, the name perhaps referring to the several salmon streams that flowed through the large swamp area behind Jericho and Locarno beaches into the ocean. Salmon were seen migrating up these streams as late as 1920.

The name Jericho is said to have evolved from a sliding together of the words Jerry's Cove. The Jerry in question was Jeremiah Rogers, who began work as a logger at Port Alberni on Vancouver Island. When this mill failed because of difficulty getting enough logs from the forests to the mills, Rogers moved to Jericho Beach and began logging what is now Kitsilano and Fairview slopes for "the best spars in the world." He was quite innovative and was one of the first loggers to use a steam-powered tractor to get logs down to English Bay or False Creek.

As early as the 1920s the government recognized the strategic impor-

Jericho air station development, ca. 1937. Photo courtesy City of Vancouver Archives.

tance of the area and began building infrastructure and fortifications along the Point Grey coast. A seaplane base was established where the Jericho Sailing Centre now sits, the big white hangar being one of the obvious legacies of this era. Flying boats were dispatched up and down the coast to do anything from chasing rum-runners to mapping the coast. Metal and chains continue to emerge from the sand to the east of the flat cement dock, presenting dangerous and sharp mementos of this era. At very low tides, the pilings used to support the hangars for seaplanes are exposed and can present a hazard for unsuspecting windsurfers and sailors.

In 1908 the new Municipality of Point Grey built a golf course in the area just east of the Sailing Centre, and in 1909 the area's first schoolhouse, a one room structure, was built. The school still stands beside Queen Mary School, the prominent red brick building high on the hillside almost directly behind the Sailing Centre.

The Vancouver Folk Music Festival, which began in 1977, is held at Jericho Park every July. Incense, tie-dyed clothes and leather sandals easily take you back in time, although now world music is as dominant as the more traditional folk sounds.

Jericho Sailing Centre Association, a friendly community-orientated organization, was established in 1974. It is a non-profit association committed to providing recreational access to English Bay for non-motorized watercraft. Its many clubs and schools teach everything from sailing and windsurfing to kayaking and seamanship. It is also home to the Disabled Sailing Centre Association of B.C., whose mission is to enrich the lives of people with significant disabilities through leisure and competitive sailing. The Sailing Centre houses The Galley restaurant, which has one of the best views in the city and some decent burgers and snacks for après paddling.

In 1976 a number of old hangars on the property were used as the base for the first UN-convened Habitat Forum. This gathering of global delegates addressed issues of urban livability and sustainability. The issues that were addressed at that time—the need for equity, human dignity, free choice, solidarity, social justice and free movement—are as relevant today as they were then. A second forum took place 20 years later in Istanbul, with a shift toward seeking answers that include development of national policies, strategies to ensure housing for all, public ownership, and planning that is comprehensive. Since 2002 the conference has been called the World Urban Forum. The Forum will once again be held in Vancouver, in June 2006, with a concurrent World Peace Forum to be sponsored by City Hall. The only visual remains of the 1976 event is a carved wooden form that is a favourite climbing site for children, found to the east of the Sailing Centre. Mysteriously, the old hangars burned down, just in time for the area to be transformed into the current park landscape.

Paddling past Jericho Sailing Centre, with Cypress and Grouse mountains in the distance

English Bay from Jericho to Wreck Beach and Log Booms – 57

Locarno Beach and Eyalmu *site, ca. 1917. Photo courtesy City of Vancouver Archives.*

As you leave Jericho, look east and you will see the Royal Vancouver Yacht Club. It was established in 1903, initially in the Stanley Park/Coal Harbour area. At that time it had 34 boats and 132 members. The Jericho site was renovated in 1978 and again in 1997. Currently there are 4,400 members, two city locations—at Coal Harbour and Jericho—and seven outstations.

Still farther east is the Jericho Tennis Club. Started in the early 1900s as a swimming and lifesaving club, it has developed into a members-only tennis club.

Farther east again is the Kitsilano Yacht Club, established in 1934. It offers recreational sailing and dinghy racing in one-design boats such as Lasers, 505s and Martin 242s. The Vancouver Parks Board's Kitsilano saltwater swimming pool is one and a half blocks east of the sailing club.

Now return to paddling west and you will pass by Locarno Beach, a westerly extension of Jericho Beach. Recently, efforts by the Vancouver Salmon and Stream Society have begun to "daylight" some of the streams that once ran to the water here, and to introduce marsh areas suitable for returning salmon. "Daylighting" is the uncovering and restoration of watercourses which, in the course of urban development, had been culverted over or made into storm drains or otherwise effaced. The society's efforts paid off in the fall of 2004 when, for the first time in over 80 years, about two dozen chum fish naturally returned to spawn at an original Vancouver salmon stream.

Locarno Beach is named after the 1925 Treaty of Locarno signed in Locarno, Switzerland, to resolve tensions resulting from the treaty that ended the First World War.

Observe the peninsula of land above Jericho and extending west that is called Point Grey. It was named after a Navy mate of Captain Vancouver.

Spanish Banks is named after the Spanish explorers Galiano and Valdes, who explored the Pacific coast and met Captain Vancouver as he was leaving Howe Sound and Jervis Inlet. The steep banks and sandy soil of the Point Grey cliffs have resulted in major erosion that occurs especially over Wreck Beach areas. Plans for managing this erosion are discussed from time to time but no action ever seems to be taken.

Much of the forested areas above the cliffs of Spanish Banks and Point Grey are the Pacific Spirit Regional Park. It has over 35 km of paths for hiking, bicycling and horseback riding as well as another 18 km exclusively for walking. The park was created from University Endowment Lands in 1989. The present name was suggested by a young girl to honour "the gateway to the Pacific and a spiritual ground to becoming one with nature."

The University Endowment Lands were given to the University of British Columbia by the province, and were to be sold and used to fund the growth of the university. As more and more green land was developed in the city, these lands became a precious resource for the area. They form a separate entity from the city and are governed by the provincial Municipal Affairs ministry.

The University of British Columbia is situated on a site called Isla de Langara by the Spanish explorer Narvaez in 1791, who appeared to think the area was an island. The university began in 1915 in huts on the Fairview slopes in False Creek. In 1922 "The

Paddlers in English Bay

English Bay from Jericho to Wreck Beach and Log Booms – 59

Great Trek" (there were no express buses in those days) saw 1,000 angry students march to Point Grey to protest their crowded classrooms and the lack of progress in developing a campus on the Endowment Lands. The current campus began development after this protest and now boasts nearly 60,000 staff and students.

Imagine being one of First People hunting in the woods above you. Deer, bear, boar and other animals were plentiful and when you looked out to the sea you knew the sea contained riches of fish, seals and otters. You will not be able to see the structure that pays tribute to this native way of life, but high above you on the University lands is the Museum of Anthropology. It was designed in 1976 by Arthur Erickson, a Vancou-ver-based, world-famous architect who also designed such structures as Simon Fraser University in Burnaby, the Vancouver Law Courts, the Waterfall Building you see as you leave Granville Island, and the Canadian Embassy in Washington, D.C., as well as various works in the Middle East. The Museum houses 535,000 ethnographic and archaeological objects from all over the world, but focuses on First Nations items, totem poles and carvings.

Acadia Beach marks the beginning of the clothing optional area of the westerly beaches.

Two cement towers will now be visible along the shore. This indicates the beginning of Tower Beach, which has the remains of two large guard/artillery towers built during

Former Second World War artillery towers are now nothing more than waterfront canvases for graffiti artists.

the Second World War to protect the harbour against attack. With ever-changing graffiti and pictures, they are now nothing more than large billboards for spray-paint artists.

Wreck Beach is Vancouver's main nude beach, with driftwood sculptures, drugs, sex and rock 'n' roll. You can see decrepit (or beautiful) bodies walking or lounging on the beach.

Log booms on the Fraser

There were many shipwrecks in the area, and even now the occasional sailboat can be seen stranded on the sandbars at low tide. In 1928, log barges, a floating grain elevator, four Second World War U.S. freighters and an ore carrier were sunk to provide a breakwater to protect the log booms close to the north arm of the Fraser River. This is probably where the name for the beach came from.

One of the many Fraser River booming grounds are ahead of you. The North Arm Jetty stretches along between the shore and the Gulf of Georgia and provides protection from the ocean waves for the log booms. Here, logs are sorted by species and rafted together to be towed to the mills along the river. Float homes provided housing in this area until as late as the 1950s for people working in the lumbering and fishing industries.

In the woods above the booming grounds, on Southwest Marine Drive, there is a plaque commemorating the arrival of Simon Fraser on July 2,

1808, after a tumultuous trip down the Fraser Canyon in search of the mouth of the Columbia River. He was an original extreme eco-adventurer, facing not only raging rivers and rapids but also angry First Nations who quite rightly were suspicious of why he was paddling up the Musqueam Creek. You can see this creek draining into the Fraser River if you paddle further east along the shore. It has recently been rehabilitated and coho and chum salmon have been successfully reintroduced.

Also in the woods above the booming grounds, there is a rookery where blue herons live, so those salmon fry may have a really short life span. On your way back to the launch site, when you see the herons flying past, you now know where at least some of them are heading.

Use the standing driftwood sentinels as your turn-about point, and unless you want an all-over suntan in an open air tanning studio, return to Jericho Beach launch site.

New Westminster from the South Shore, ca. 1850s. Photo courtesy Vancouver Public Library.

A BRIEF HISTORY OF NEW WESTMINSTER

THE HISTORY OF NEW WESTMINSTER and the history of the Fraser River go hand in hand. First Nations settlements, gold prospectors, salmon, paddle wheelers and fur-trading forts all benefited from the river, whether for transportation or for the bounty it yielded. As with any river, the Fraser, over the years, was shaped by and helped shape the people who lived and worked along its banks.

The Fraser River has been designated a Heritage River by the governments of both British Columbia and Canada. It is one of five drainage systems within British Columbia. As a watershed, it is, at 231,510 square

History continues on p. 64

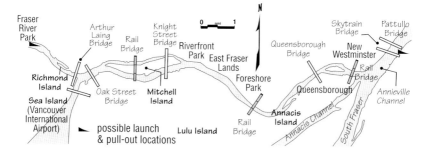

Fraser River Park — Arthur Laing Bridge — Rail Bridge — Knight Street Bridge — Riverfront Park — East Fraser Lands — Skytrain Bridge — Pattullo Bridge — Queensborough Bridge — New Westminster — Richmond Island — Oak Street Bridge — Mitchell Island — Foreshore Park — Queensborough — Rail Bridge — Annieville Channel — Sea Island (Vancouver International Airport) — Annacis Island — Annacis Channel — South Fraser

0   nmi   1
N

possible launch
& pull-out locations   Lulu Island   Rail Bridge

4 New Westminster to Fraser River Park

Difficulty Intermediate conditions – moderate risk

Distance 12 nmi one way

Duration 3–3.5 hours on an outgoing tide. The total trip will take about 6 hours, including dropping off and picking up vehicles.

Charts 3489 Fraser River, Pattullo Bridge to Crescent Island, 1:20,000
3490 Fraser River, Sand Heads to Douglas Island, 1:20,000
3491 Fraser River, North Arm, 1:20,000

Launch site

Located in between the Pattullo and Skytrain bridges that connect New Westminster and Surrey, Brownsville Bar Park on the south shore of the Fraser River is an out-of-the-way spot popular primarily for fishing. It is an easy 100-m carry down a bark path to a sandy beach. There are no easily accessible launch points close to New Westminster on the north shore of the Fraser River.

Take-out site

The suggested take-out site is at the Fraser River Park in the Marpole area of South Vancouver. East Vancouver's Riverfront Park at the end of Kerr Street provides an option to shorten the trip by about half. McDonald Beach Park, located on Sea Island, is also a good alternative, but will add both driving and paddling time to the trip.

Getting there

This trip requires two vehicles or someone to drop you off and pick you up at the end of the trip.

If you are using two vehicles, drop the first one off at Fraser River Park in South Vancouver. Access is from Southwest Marine Drive, two blocks west of Granville Street. Turn south onto Barnard Street and continue south until you meet West 75th Avenue. Turn right and continue until you see the park on your left. The take-out is at the far end of the park, so leave your vehicle in the westernmost parking lot.

***Guide* continues on p. 65**

kilometres, more than twice as big as the next largest river, the Columbia, and it drains about one quarter of British Columbia. Beginning at Moose Lake near Mount Robson, it flows 1,399 kilometres to the Pacific Ocean, the longest river to have its course totally within British Columbia. This enormous basin of the Fraser encompasses nearly 65 per cent of the province's population and 48 per cent of its farmland.

New Westminster is a major city on the banks of the Fraser, often referred to as the "Royal City." It received this nickname after Queen Victoria chose the reference to the site of the English Parliament at Westminster over the name Queensborough, which had been suggested by the new colony. The other, less recognized connection to the name "Royal" is the contribution the Royal Engineers made to the early establishment of the city.

In 1858 the Royal Engineers, Columbia Division, commanded by Colonel Richard Moody, were sent to British Columbia to begin surveying the colony and to maintain peace and order in the gold mining towns. In 1859 they arrived at Sapperton, slightly east of present-day New Westminster, and for the next four years the engineers cleared and surveyed the New Westminster townsite to prepare it to be the new capital of the mainland colony. Sapperton got its name from the shovels, or "saps," used by the military engineers, or "sappers." At the same time as laying out the neat, numbered streets of New Westminster, the soldiers constructed wharves along the city front and the "wagon road" to the Cariboo. As well, trails were cut to link New Westminster to the developing town of Granville (Vancouver) on Burrard Inlet. By 1864 funding for this force was depleted and the soldiers either stayed on as settlers in the area or returned to England.

History continues on p. 66

After returning to Southwest Marine Drive you have two options to get to Brownsville: continuing on Marine Drive to the Pattullo Bridge; or travel via the Richmond Highway, across the Alex Fraser Bridge to Delta and Surrey. The day's traffic reports may assist you in choosing the fastest route.

From the Pattullo Bridge, take the Scott Road exit. Continue straight on Scott Road for about 400 m. Turn right onto Old Yale Road. You will be heading northeast. Continue to the end of Old Yale Road. The park is across the railway tracks to the right.

From the Alex Fraser Bridge, take the Nordel Way exit toward River Road. Take Nordel back toward the Fraser River until it runs into River Road. Turn east on River Road. It will soon become South Fraser Way. After crossing under the Skytrain bridge, turn left onto Old Yale Road and continue to the end of the road. The park is across the railway tracks to the right.

For a shorter trip, use Riverfront Park at the extreme south end of Kerr Street in Vancouver as your take-out location. Access is easy: simply turn south onto Kerr Street, which is 1.2 km west of Boundary Road and about 1.5 km east of Victoria Drive.

Parking

There is a small free parking lot at Brownsville Bar Park. Make sure you do not leave any valuables in your vehicle here. It may be advisable to inquire about parking in the pub parking lot you passed just before crossing the railway tracks if you are going to take your time doing the trip. Parking at Fraser River park is also free. If you park in the westernmost lot, you will be closest to the take-out.

Washrooms

There is a porta-potty near the Brownsville Park. As well, there are washrooms in the Burnaby Fraser Foreshore Park, but there is not an easy pull-out location here. Riverfront Park in East Vancouver and about halfway along the route has washrooms and an easy pull-out. There are also washrooms in the Fraser River Park at the end of the trip.

Paddling considerations

This is not a trip for beginners or those not confident in steep or following waves. The presence of log booms along the shore and frequent tugs and other working boats creates the challenge of staying out of the way of boats but not getting close to the booms, which you could become trapped beneath if you were to capsize. The North Fraser Port Authority states that tugs and other river craft work every day all day, so going on the weekend will not ensure any less traffic. The Fraser is a "working river." For the most part, the tugboat pilots are courteous when it comes to paddlers, but no matter how slow tugs may go, they create heavy, steep waves when they pass. In addition there can be speeding pleasure motorboats, floating logs and debris, fast flowing water, currents and eddies.

The route

You are launching at a site that has a history little known to the general

Guide continues on p. 67

New Westminster's first city market day after the Great Fire of 1898.
Photo courtesy New Westminster Public Library.

New Westminster owes thanks to the Royal Engineers' energy and vision, which resulted in its being western Canada's oldest city and, in 1866, the first capital of the United Colonies of British Columbia. Although New Westminster retained the capital city honour for only two years, as Victoria was named the capital in 1868, the name "Royal City" has been used to advantage ever since for promoting the city's image.

Despite losing the prestige of being the capital, the new city developed well, with nearby communities supplying produce and buying needed goods. In 1892, a City Market was built along the waterfront to accommodate this commerce. As well, salmon canning, lumbering, metal works, a grain company and a woollen mill contributed a large part to the economy. In September 1898, a fire ravaged three-quarters of the city, the

History continues on p. 68

public. The Qw'ontl'en (Kwantlen) First Nations for many years had a village called Quqqa':yt (Kikait) in the same area where, in 1860, Ebenezer Brown purchased land. He built a wharf and a hotel, which resulted in Brown's Landing becoming a rest stop for people crossing the river to New Westminster. By 1887 Brown's Landing was called Brownsville, and by 1890 there were five hotels, a general store, a livery stable and a blacksmith shop in the area. A steam ferry called the *Knivet de Knevit*, built by Captain Grant and probably named after his niece Kate de Nevit, operated from here to take produce and passengers across to the city and bring goods back. Farmers also used the ferry to take grain to the Fort Langley mill. The town's growth was helped by the fact it was at the convergence of the Kirkland and Scott Roads to Ladner, the Semiahmoo Road from Blaine, and the Yale Road to the Fraser Valley. The Yale Road, today called the Old Yale Road, is the same one you drove on to the launch today. When the Fraser River toll bridge for vehicles and trains was built in 1904, it bypassed Brownsville and the town rapidly lost its importance.

The Pattullo Bridge, to the east of you, was often called the "Pay-toll-o" bridge, because it was initially a toll bridge when it opened in 1937. It has not been upgraded and each of its three lanes is only three metres wide—which is two feet narrower than the safety standards of today—and make the Pattullo one of the most hazardous bridges in the Lower Mainland.

Guide continues on p. 69

Pattullo and Skytrain bridges spanning the Fraser River

market, wharves and the ships docked there, as well as to the south toward the u.s. border and as far north as the Fraser Valley. Despite many of the main buildings on the main commercial street—Columbia Street—being made of brick and stone, only two buildings survived. One of these was the Guichon Hotel (you can read about the Guichon family in Trip 9, Deas Slough).

Immediately after the fire, the city began to rebuild and by 1910 was firmly re-established. It continued to make slow and steady progress in establishing industries, but experienced a very large increase in building and real-estate markets.

New Westminster's connection by the Skytrain to Surrey and Vancouver in 1986 echoed the electric inter-urban line built in 1891. While separated by 100 years, both of these transportation lines meant increased access to Vancouver and therefore a positive influence on the economy of New Westminster.

The early development of New Westminster and surrounding communities is historically interesting, of course, but there is another reason why this route is included in this book: it is one of the oldest historic marine trails in the Lower Mainland. It was on July 2, 1808, that Simon Fraser, intrepid explorer for the North West Company, reached the mouth of the Fraser River in his search to find a water route to the Pacific and the mouth of the Columbia River. He left Fort St. James in May of 1808 with 21 North West Company employees and two First Nations guides, all loaded into four canoes. Like an original *Survivor* trip, the group faced raging rapids, impassable canyons, treacherous whirlpools and hostile natives. In some places along the Upper Fraser they had to walk along canyon walls on ladders built from ropes and trees and clamber endlessly up and down small ledges. Canoes disintegrated and natives who had been persuaded to "lend" their canoes to the party of explorers

History continues on p. 70

The Fraser River just east of the Oak Street Bridge is still largely a working river.

The other bridge you see above you as you launch is the Skytrain Bridge. At the time it was built in 1986, it was the world's longest cable-supported transit-only bridge.

As you begin to paddle, just before the river divides, you can see on the south shore a park called Tannery Park. Obviously at one time there was a tannery in this area, but there was also, along the river, a small community of Norwegians who lived on scow houseboats and fished and worked in New Westminster.

Paddle west along the south shore of the river until you are opposite downtown New Westminster. Check for barges and tugboats and then cross over to the city waterfront. As you look back you will see ocean freight-ers moored along the shore. These vessels represent a small fraction of the commerce that passes through the transportation corridor admin-istered by the Fraser River Port Au-thority. The total national economic value resulting from port activities is $5.3 billion per year and growing. The port is Canada's second largest and North America's second largest automobile port. Over 770 deep-sea ships enter the port, with vehicles (445,000 in 2003), forest products, containers and steel being the main imports and exports.

New Westminster Quay and Market is where you should arrive after the crossing. The public market opened in August 1985 and has been a "gathering place"—the First Nations

Guide **continues on p. 71**

became angry. Despite these incessant hardships and near-death experiences, Fraser, who was described as "inured to hardship; versed in woodcraft and the lore of the savage; strong in danger; of unconquerable will and energy; unlettered, but true to his friends and honourable in his dealings," was certainly not going to be the one voted off the expedition! So he persevered, and arrived at the mouth of the river in July—just in time for the summer salmon run and to be greeted by a suspicious Musqueam First Nation. Fraser left hastily and discouraged, for he had not discovered the mouth of the Columbia and thus was unable to claim it for Britain; his goal for the entire trip was thwarted. On an equally exhausting 34-day trip back to Fort George he surpassed his 35-day downstream voyage by one day. While he continued to work in the fur trade for another ten years, he eventually retired to farming near Cornwall, Ontario.

So this was the man, and this is the legacy that you are following when you kayak down this great river named after its most famous explorer.

❧

The sternwheeler snagboat Sampson I, *ca. 1884. Photo courtesy New Westminster Public Library.*

interpretation of the word "quay"—ever since. The City Market of the late 1800s was also situated along the wharf, as were industries such as sawmills and the Royal City Cannery at the foot of the Pattullo Bridge.

On the east side of the quay, hidden behind the larger-than-life riverboat casino, is the Fraser River Discovery Centre, which opened in 2001. Its mission is to "take a key leadership role in enhancing the health and sustainability of the Fraser River by enlightening and educating individuals of all ages and cultures about the economic, natural historic, aesthetic and spiritual worth of the Fraser River and its basin."

The rest of the city waterfront is now dominated by the floating casino, a modern paddlewheeler used for river cruises, shops and, to the far east, a very large, unattractive concrete carpark. The carpark opened in 1959 in a misguided attempt to keep shoppers in the downtown core and away from the newly developed malls; unfortunately it means you have little chance of seeing from the water any of the older buildings on Front Street.

However, you can see the paddlewheeler *Sampson V* moored at the quay as a permanent historic display. This boat was the last steam-powered paddlewheeler to operate on the Fraser. It was built in 1937 for the federal government and, like the four preceding *Sampson*s, had been a snagpuller. This meant that its crew searched the river for deadheads—floating logs and other debris that could create hazards—and removed as much as they could. Paddlewheelers were used as transportation and for recreation between 1836, when the first Hudson's Bay Company sidewheeler, the *Beaver*, began working the B.C. coast, and 1980, when the *Sampson V* retired. At one time, when steam paddlewheelers were the main transportation on the river between New Westminster and Yale—the farthest east they went in the lower Fraser Valley—there were more paddlewheelers on the Fraser than on the Mississippi. The completion of the CPR through to Vancouver contributed to the rapid decline of this form of transportation except on a few inland rivers and lakes.

The Inn at the Quay, attached to the quay complex, seems designed to have the appearance of a large riverboat ready to take its guests for a cruise.

Paddle off in a westerly direction, keeping well to the right side of the river but always staying away from the moored log booms. You are about to paddle under five bridges, past four municipalities, see numerous sawmills with bobbing baby tugs manoeuvring logs into the mill, shipyards, paper mills, boatworks, fish plants, a cement plant, fronts or backs of industrial complexes and on the north shore an increasing number of apartments and townhouses.

So, let's go! After you pass under the Queensborough railway bridge the river will be divided by Poplar Island, a regional legacy site. Pass it on the left, as the channel to the right is overly industrialized. On your left is Lulu Island. It was named in 1863 after a visiting 16-year-old U.S. actress,

Lulu Sweet, who so impressed the female-starved loggers, fishermen and soldiers, that Colonel Moody himself, of Royal Engineers fame, is said to have named the island after her.

The majority of this low-lying island is the Municipality of Richmond and is covered with housing, commercial buildings and industry, although 48 km^2 has been maintained in an agricultural land reserve as a recognition of its history.

The Queensborough car bridge is next. It retains the suggested name for the city that was rejected by Queen Victoria in favour of New Westminster. From 1891 to 1913 the bridge was a trestle built to connect Lulu Island with New Westminster. It crosses to the suburb of Queensborough on Lulu Island and Annacis Island Industrial Estate.

On the south shore of the river you will pass by two fishing bar parks—Tree Island before the Canadian National Railway swing bridge, and #9 Road Fish Bar. Judging by the number of people fishing here during salmon runs, these continue to be respectable fishing sites, despite reduced salmon numbers, and no doubt were part of the reason why the First Nations lived close to this area.

The bounty of the river in the form of salmon contributed to, in the 1880s, the canning of salmon becoming the second largest industry in British Columbia after mining. There are seven species of salmon that swim in the Pacific Ocean, with sockeye, pink, chum, chinook (spring) and coho being the most common. Canning of the fish began near New Westminster in 1867, with initially only chinook and chum being processed. By 1918 there were 80 canneries operating along the coast, with 223 cannery sites developed overall. In 1999, eight salmon canneries and 190 fish processing plants speak to the fact of both increased efficiency and a vastly diminished resource.

Paddle on while you think about fish, since beneath your kayak a large sturgeon may be swimming. Although none have been captured recently that are the size of the fish caught in the late 1800s, which could weigh over 450 kilos, comparatively large ones of 180 kilos or so have occasionally been taken. So perhaps another caution is in order: beware of the river sturgeon. Even at today's modest size of about 180 kilos, this is a fish with which you probably do not want to swim.

On your right, past the big right-hand bend in the river, is Burnaby's Fraser Foreshore Park. Annoyingly, no consideration was given to accessing the water, making its washrooms and picnic tables impossible to reach without climbing up steep banks and over slippery rocks.

The park is followed by a large, empty, post-industrial area where a Weyerhaeuser forestry complex used to stand. This vacant lot, on what is called the East Fraserlands, is slated to be developed into a new community with as many as 15 high-rise towers and single-family homes and townhomes to house up to 15,000 people.

Vancouver's broad Riverfront Park is next. This is the best location to pull out for a snack and to stretch your legs. Just beyond a well-maintained walking jetty, and hidden in a gap between

Beneath your kayak a large sturgeon may be swimming! This one, caught in April 1925, measured 12'8" and weighed 1,015 lb. Photo courtesy New Westminster Public Library.

log booms, you will find a fine gravel beach to land on. Those who need to use the washroom will have to hustle about 200 m to the west past the tennis courts to the public facilities.

This is also the best location to stop for a shorter-length trip. Access is via Kerr Street, south of Marine Drive.

After you pass the park, if you stay to the right as you pass Mitchell Island, you will have less chance of meeting a container ship and its ensuing wake. Mitchell Island is devoted to industry and to offloading and storing of the contents of container ships. It is accessed via the Knight Street Bridge, built in 1974, which you will now paddle under. The bridge and street are named after Robert Knight, an early South Vancouver landowner.

The next bridge you will pass under is the Oak Street Bridge, opened in 1957. It is an extension of one of the many streets named after local trees by Canadian Pacific Railway surveyor Lauchlan Hamilton in the late 1800s. It was a toll bridge until 1959 and replaced the swing bridge from Marpole that previously spanned the North Arm. A little-used CPR swing bridge continues to run parallel to the Oak Street Bridge.

The North Fraser Port Authority offices are on the point of land just before you go under the final bridge. The Arthur Laing Bridge is the most recently constructed on this route. The Alex Fraser Bridge on the South Fraser is newer, having been built in 1986, but you only see it from the launch site and do not go under it. A bridge from Marpole was at the same location where the Arthur Laing Bridge was built in 1975 as an extension of Granville Street. The Arthur Laing provides a rapid route to Richmond and the airport, situated on Sea Island. It was named after a British Columbia politician who was once the leader of the provincial Liberal Party. Between 1962 and 1972 he served in the House of Commons and was later appointed a Senator.

Sea Island is the home of the Vancouver Airport. In the 1860s it had an early history of agriculture, with a farm owned by Hugh McRoberts expanding to be the largest in the British Empire. There also was a small community called Eburne on the northeast corner, where a hotel and cannery stood.

This way of life came to an end when Vancouver International Airport (YVR) opened in 1931 and replaced a smaller airport that had been on Lulu Island. The airport was owned by the city of Richmond until 1962, when

SS Beaver
carrying
Sons of Scotland
to a picnic at
Langley, ca. 1906.
Photo courtesy
New Westminster
Public Library.

it was bought by the federal Department of Transport. In 1992 the Airport Authority took over management and operation of the airport and embarked upon major renovations in all areas. The airport is now Canada's second busiest, with 250,400 take-offs and landings in 2003 and 14.3 million passengers passing through. It also wins praise and awards for being an attractive, welcoming environment, with art and sculptures adorning hallways and arrivals, departures and waiting areas.

You are nearing the end of your trip. The pull-out spot can be identified by the park benches and boardwalk along the water and a small sandy beach that is available, if the tide is not too high, at the extreme west end of the park.

In 1876, long before it became a park, this area was the farm of Samuel McCleery, an Irishman who raised cattle and grew hay and vegetables. Two marsh-grass islands near the Fraser River pier were also part of his property, but they have long since disappeared, eroded by the forces of the ever-changing river. The nearby McCleery Golf Course is named after this early settler.

After you pull out your boat, it is worthwhile to walk around the park and read the informative signs about river life and the natural history of the area. Then return to your launch site to pick up your other vehicle.

Looking west along the North Fraser from the Trip 4 take-out point

Dance hall at Deep Cove, circa early 1900s. Photo courtesy Deep Cove Heritage Society.

AN BRIEF BUT IN-DEPTH HISTORY OF DEEP COVE, ROCHE POINT (CATES PARK) AND BELCARRA

INDIAN ARM IS A 30-KILOMETRE-LONG FJORD that has over 40 creeks and streams emptying into it. In the colder 1800s, because of this inflow of fresh water, the northern end of the Arm would often freeze over in the winter.

The lands at the mouth of Indian Arm were a living and food-gathering site for the Tsleil-Waututh (People of the Inlet) for many generations. Numerous middens have been identified and many artifacts recovered from this area. For over 3,000 years, the area that is now Belcarra

History continues on p. 78

5 Deep Cove to Cates Park, Belcarra Park and Jug Island

Difficulty Beginner conditions – low risk

Distance 6.5 nmi

Duration 3 hours round trip

Charts 3311 Sunshine Coast—Vancouver Harbour to Desolation Sound, 1:40,000
3494 Vancouver Harbour, Central Portion, 1:10,000;
Second Narrows 1:6,000
3495 Vancouver Harbour, Eastern Portion, 1:10,000; Indian Arm, 1:30,000

Launching and take-out sites

The best launch site is from the beach in Deep Cove immediately beside the Deep Cove Canoe and Kayak rental location. Their building also contains change facilities and washrooms. Access is easy and there are plenty of amenities nearby to have a bite to eat before or after your paddle. It is also possible to launch at either Cates Park or Barnet Marine Park.

Getting there

Deep Cove is accessed from either Mount Seymour Parkway or the Dollarton Highway. Exit east from the #1 Highway to either of these roads. Follow Mount Seymour Parkway for about 5.5 km or Dollarton Highway for about 7 km until their junction with Deep Cove Road. The landmark Raven Pub is a few buildings in from the intersection and is a great place for an après paddle drink. Follow Deep Cove Road north for 1.2 km until the road swings right and turns into Gallant Road. Go to the end of Gallant Road and turn right onto Banbury Road. About 100 m along on the left of Banbury Road is the public access to Deep Cove. There is a loading area right beside the beach.

Cates Park is accessed directly from the Dollarton Highway, about 6 km east of Highway 1 on the south side of the road. It is well signed.

Barnet Marine Park is located south of the Barnet Highway on the north side of Burnaby Mountain. From Burnaby take Hastings Street east until it turns into the Barnet Highway. Follow the signs to the park.

Parking

Deep Cove—There is plenty of free parking in lots parallel to Rockcliff Street to the south of Deep Cove and in Panorama Park to the west of the cove. Overnight parking is not permitted, however. If you park on the street, be aware of local parking restrictions.
Cates Park—in parking lot.
Barnet Park—in parking lot.

Washrooms

There are washrooms and change rooms located in the Deep Cove Canoe and Kayak building in Deep Cove and in Panorama Park to the north of the Deep Cove launch site, Cates Park, Barnet Park, Belcarra Park main park area, Maple Beach and Jug Island Beach (opposite Jug Island).

Guide continues on p. 79

Park was their main winter village, called Tum-tumay-whueton—"biggest place for people, good land"—and was shared with Squamish and Musqueam tribes in the summer. There were cod, halibut, herring, oolichan, perch, salmon, smelt, sole, trout, sturgeon, crabs and mussels readily available year round. In the forests and sea, deer, mountain goat, elk, bear, beaver, otter, mink and seal were abundant. Berries, plants, roots and herbs were used for food, clothing and medicine.

Captain Vancouver entered the area of Burrard Inlet in 1792 but did not sail up Indian Arm. That same year, the Spanish captains Galiano and Valdes were also in Burrard Inlet and did sail up the fjord, observed the native living areas and named the area Canal de Sasamat, meaning "a cool place" from the native word "Tsaatsmat."

It took over 65 years before the area was "rediscovered" when, in 1859, Captain George Henry Richards from the New Westminster-based Royal Navy, was mapping the area and looking for suitable locations for a military post. Many islands and mainland places throughout the region are still known today by the names Captain Richards gave them.

The encroachment of white settlers into the area between 1858 and 1864 resulted in the natives moving to two areas, one that was to become the Burrard Reserve, the other at the end of Indian Arm near where the Wigwam Inn was eventually built. After Canada was established as the Dominion of Canada in 1867, a reserve system was more formally initiated and 111 acres was set aside on the north shore of Burrard Inlet (east of the Second Narrows Bridge) for use by the Tsleil-Waututh (Burrard) First Nation.

Deep Cove was once called "Deepwater" because of its deep harbour and surrounding waters. Limestone quarrying and logging encouraged settlement in the early years.

History continues on p. 80

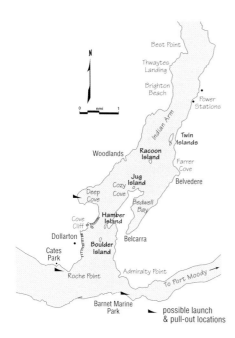

Map labels:
N

Best Point
Thwaytes Landing
Brighton Beach
Power Stations
Indian Arm
Twin Islands
Woodlands
Racoon Island
Farrer Cove
Jug Island
Cozy Cove
Belvedere
Deep Cove
Bedwell Bay
Cove Cliff
Hamber Island
Dollarton
Boulder Island
Belcarra
Cates Park
Roche Point
Admiralty Point
To Port Moody
Barnet Marine Park

0   nmi   1

➤ possible launch
& pull-out locations

Paddling considerations

Expect heavy motorized boat traffic in the summer, especially near the Deep Cove Marina on the north side of Deep Cove and in the middle of Indian Arm. Be extra aware of pleasure boats in the Grey Rock Island/Hamber Island/Boulder Island area. The channel is at its narrowest here and boats are funnelled into this passage from all directions. On warm summer days a predictable anabatic (inflow) wind blows from the south up Indian arm. In the colder months, the opposite can occur, with a strong outflow wind blowing from the north and whipping up stormy conditions. Freighters heading to the oil terminals, water skiers, divers and stronger currents around Hamber Island and Turtlehead should also be kept in mind when planning your trip. Do not attempt to paddle west of Cates Park toward the Second Narrows Bridge. Currents can reach 6 knots with steep choppy waves and large eddies close to shore in this area.

The route

Paddle out of the Deep Cove area, noting the varied West Coast architecture, steps and elevator mechanisms that adapt to the steep cliffs on which the houses perch. One little yellow house close to the water remains as a

Guide continues on p. 81

Deep Cove to Cates Park, Belcarra Park and Jug Island – 79

In the 1900s there was an influx of miners after gold was discovered in the Seymour Creek area. Unfortunately, the dreams were much larger than the small flakes of gold that were found, and mining in the area was short-lived.

Although it would be a long time before an overland route to Deep Cove would be built, the tranquil setting of Deep Cove and Indian Arm helped it become a popular summer destination. Frequent arrivals of the New Brighton Ferry Service (1908 to 1920) dropped off happy people to stay at the Quarries Lodge located on the Deep Cove shore under Lookout Rock, or to their small summer cabins. Others came to dance up a storm in the hall overlooking the Deep Cove beach or in the Belcarra Park area. These boats also brought supplies and mail to the lumber camps farther up Indian Arm.

In 1920 the ferry company was sold to Captain J.D. Stalker and became the Harbour Navigation Company. The *Scenic*, the *Hollyburn* and the *Harbour Princess*

History continues on p. 82

The Dollar lumber mill at Dollarton/Deep Cove, circa 1915. Photo courtesy Deep Cove Heritage Society.

reminder of the small summer homes that were common when Deep Cove was mainly a summer destination. Round the point, keeping to your right.

You will pass a rock, now called Grey Rock but previously called White Rock when Captain Richards surveyed the area in 1859–60. The Tsleil-Waututh people call it Spuka-nah-ah.

Above you is Cove Cliff, where various movie stars have rented homes to escape the madding crowds of Vancouver. Paddling in this area offers the opportunity to wave to homeowners, note the different kinds of liquid refreshments people drink while on their dock patios, the types of dockside chairs they use, and the number of homes that have kayaks as well as motor launches. (Quite a few, actually.)

One especially imposing home, at 828 Beachview Drive, has a waterside tennis court, a two-floor, semi-circular, floor-to-roof window, large lawns and an air of mystery. Who does it belong to? A movie star, royalty, an oil baron?

The Dollarton area, where the large Dollar and Cypress lumber mills used to stand, is now a residential area and includes Cates Park.

When Cates Park first appears, if you wish to land, continue paddling until you come to the main beach shore at Roche Point, where there is better access to the park.

Roche Point was named after Lieutenant Richard Roche who patrolled the North West coast in the 1850s in HMS *Satellite*. In the early 1900s a plan was presented to turn the area into a major industrial location with a world-class dock and shipyard and a company town to be called Roslyn. Although a formal agreement with the federal government was in the works, the project did not receive enough subsidies to progress.

The Cates Park area is called Whey-ah-whichen ("facing the wind") by the Tsleil-Waututh. The name describes where Indian Arm begins and Burrard Inlet ends and aptly describes the weather you frequently face when you paddle in Indian Arm.

The park is 23.5 hectares in size and in 1950 was named after Captain Charles Cates, the founder of Cates Towing Company. The Cates family is a perfect case study for nature vs. nurture questions. Charles was one of five brothers who were all master mariners, and all three of Captain Cates's own sons ended up as sea captains and members of the family that contributed substantially to the social and political life of the North Shore and the province.

If you want to have a walk about in the park, you can see the remains of the old burner from the Dollar sawmill, a totem pole and a 50-foot war canoe that took the late Chief Henry Peter George over a year to carve by hand. Along its edge it has a checkerboard design which led to the name "Old Checkerboard." As well, there is an anchor from a sailboat that used to come into the inlet, which the Cates family donated to the park.

Wooden sailing boats were deliberately taken further up Indian Arm to sit for several days. Because there

Guide continues on p. 83

Deep Cove to Cates Park, Belcarra Park and Jug Island – 81

transported people up the Inlet. For $2 you could have a four-hour cruise to Wigwam Inn and return trip to Vancouver. In the 1960s the company was purchased by Harbour Ferries, and in 1996 its name changed yet again, to Harbour Cruises Ltd. A new *Harbour Princess* continues the tradition of scenic cruises up Indian Arm.

Dollarton, Roche Point and Cates Park were first developed around 1877 when loggers saw the opportunities for employment and wealth presented by the large trees on the north shores. The largest tree felled in the area was a 126.5-metre giant cut down in 1902 near North Vancouver's Lynn Valley.

By 1914, two sawmills, Cedarside Mill and Robert Dollar's Dollar Mill, had been built and the community of "Dollar Town" had sprung up, with docks, a community hall, and a school in the Roche Point area. The children from Deep Cove either walked along an old deer trail through the woods or rowed the same route that you will take in your kayak, to get to the area's only school, located in the Dollarton area.

The Great Depression beginning in 1929 resulted in both of the lumber mills closing and the people of Deep Cove and Dollarton struggling to find employment.

It wasn't until after the Second World War that Deep Cove again began to attract businesses and home-owners. Since that time, with its ready access to city life, it has once more recaptured its reputation as a peaceful, beautiful area in which to live.

Belcarra was named by Judge Bole, who used the spot as a summer retreat. The name is from two Celtic words meaning "fair land upon which the sun shines." Like Deep Cove, Belcarra became a resort, with a long wharf for ferry docking, summer resort cabins and a dance hall. It was readily accessible by the various stern-

History continues on p. 84

Deep Cove kayakers, 2004

were more streams and runoff into the Arm in those days, the seawater had a large proportion of fresh water mixed into it, which killed off the barnacles that would otherwise be munching away on the wooden hulls.

Malcolm Lowry, a renowned Canadian author (both for his ability to drink vast quantities of liquor and for writing such influential novels as *Under the Volcano*) lived from 1940 to 1954 in one of the shacks in the woods at Cates Park. A walk in the northeast park is named after him, the

Malcolm Lowry Walk. These squatters' shacks had originally housed workmen, lumbermen and fishermen looking for cheap accommodation. Drawn by the remoteness and beauty of the setting, other Canadian writers such as Dorothy Livesay, Earle Birney and Sandy Frances Duncan followed Lowry's example and made use of the shacks as summer retreats.

Nowadays you probably won't hear poetry readings, but on summer weekend afternoons you may hear a concert in the park, with various

Guide continues on p. 85

Deep Cove to Cates Park, Belcarra Park and Jug Island – 83

wheelers and small boats that transported supplies and passengers up the Arm. In the early 1900s a portion of the Belcarra area was purchased from Captain Cates, who was then owner of Harbour Navigation and the Belcarra land, and the present-day Regional Park was created.

With improved access to water and the building of the first official roads into the Belcarra area in 1952, thousands of tourists had access to Belcarra, Sasamat and Buntzen Lakes and to the subdivisions that began to be planned. Still, even in the early 1970s, places like Turtlehead had more of a track than a road as their only access to the homes. Today the roads to the area bring thousands of day trippers and tourists to enjoy the beaches, hikes and spectacular views in the Belcarra area.

Beach and Deep Cove Yacht Club at bottom right, circa 1937. Photo courtesy Deep Cove Heritage Society.

styles of music being played by local musicians.

In 1865 in the Cates Park area, Hugh Burr planted fruit trees, raised cattle and established the first farm and dairy. He rowed over to Hastings townsite, Moodyville (Lower Lonsdale area) and even travelled as far as New Westminster to sell his produce. When sailing lumber ships were in the Inlet, he had shore-to-ship service ready to supply them.

In the distance you can see the Second Narrows Bridge, one of the seven bridges connecting downtown Vancouver to the various surrounding districts. The homesteaders on the North Shore had to row or canoe back and forth to Vancouver. Later a ferry service began between Vancouver and North Vancouver, but the journey by land from North Vancouver to the Deep Cove area was still arduous with bridge washouts and treacherous roads. Eventually in 1925 a wooden bridge, with a railway down the middle, one-way, single-lane traffic on either side and a sidewalk on the east side, was built in the area where the Second Narrows Bridge is located today. The bridge had a lift span so ships could pass into the inlet. This span of course was supposed to be in the deep, centre channel, but to keep costs down it was put closer to the south end of the bridge. This led to a number of boat-meets-bridge incidents and the need for reconstruction. Another bridge was eventually built in 1934, and although its financing contributed to the bankruptcy of the City and District of North Vancouver,

it did help increase the population of the North Shore and Deep Cove areas by easing access to them.

The official name of the six-lane bridge you now see is the Ironworkers Memorial Second Narrows Crossing, in memory of the steelworkers who died during the collapse of a middle section during initial construction in 1957. It is generally called the Second Narrows Bridge, although signs posted at either end of the bridge use the full name to remind drivers of the fragility of steel and human life.

In 1912 a group of engineers had plans for building a dam across the inlet at Second Narrows, with locks to gain access to the upper lake. This would have created a freshwater lake from the North Arm (Indian Arm) where boats could moor and lose their barnacles. A roadbed for trains and a tram was to run along the top. Both this plan and a similar one broached in 1931 were turned down by the governments of the day.

Looking across to the south shore, you can see an abandoned, multi-level, silver-coloured barge. Anyone who attended Expo 86 probably went aboard this barge at least once, because it is the famous McBarge—a McDonald's fast food outlet that floated in False Creek during the fair. After Expo the barge was put up for sale in hopes it could be recycled into something useful but no plans ever evolved. Eventually it was towed to its present location.

East of McBarge you will see numerous oil storage tanks. Imperial Oil purchased the land in 1911, from the

Indian Arm

same German land baron who bought and finished the construction of the Wigwam Inn. By 1921 the company had built its plant and the company town of Ioco on the north side of Burrard Inlet. The deep-sea port provided ready access for oil tankers, and Imperial was later joined by Petro-Canada and Chevron in developing this area.

On the side of the forested hill nestles the puffy roof of the Burnaby Velodrome, which is owned by the City of Burnaby and was built by Cycling BC between 1991 and 1997. It is the only indoor velodrome in Canada.

The track is 200 m long by 6 m wide, with a 47-degree slope at its steepest curves. Think you can cycle fast? To remain upright on this track you have to pedal at least 30 km/h.

High on the south shore is Simon Fraser University. It was designed by Arthur Erickson and opened in 1965. Concrete construction, numerous levels and long, low, clean lines mark the architectural style. SFU continues to enjoy a reputation as an innovative and free-thinking institution with a world-class location. There are recent plans for development of a vast housing complex called UniverCity Highlands below the ring road surrounding the university academic buildings. The City of Burnaby received 332 hectares of university land outside the ring road to preserve in its natural form, in return for approval to build 1,800 homes during the next 7 to 10 years and a total of 4,500 within the next 20 years.

Early weekday mornings and after work hours you may see the Westcoast Express zooming along faster than the cars on the Barnet Highway. It is a commuter train that runs from Mission City to Vancouver downtown waterfront, taking 73 minutes to complete the 68-km trip.

Barnet Marine Park, directly opposite Admiralty Point in Belcarra Park, provides an additional area to launch your kayak for the Deep Cove trips if you arrive from the eastern part of the Lower Mainland.

You now have two choices to continue your route. You can go back the way you came along the shore and cross to the east side at Boulder Island, or you can carefully cross the mouth of Indian Arm to Admiralty Point in Belcarra Regional Park. If you choose the latter route, be aware of cross-chop waves and wash from the numerous motorboats heading up the Arm. Also, this is a fairly long, open stretch of water exposed to the many wind variations in Indian Arm/Burrard Inlet. There is a white shell beach at Admiralty Point at low tide and a landing spot at Maple Beach, to the north of the Point, with a washroom. Further north is a small promontory called Cod Rock, where you will often find adults and children fishing.

Boulder Island was used by the Tsleil-Waututh (People of the Inlet) as a sacred burial site of their first chief Waut-salk. After members of the tribe converted to Christianity, the chief was reburied in the cemetery on the Burrard reserve. Two orca whales were said to have accompanied his canoe as his body made this journey. Orcas are seldom seen in Indian Arm these days, but if they are, it is believed they too are there to accompany a departing spirit. The island is now private land. At one time there was an 18-tonne granite boulder on the island. A story is told that one day when the fog was very thick, a tugboat, drill and scow came to drag it away for use as anchors to moor log booms. When the fog lifted, the boats and the rock were gone, and it is believed that the remaining rock fell into the ocean and broke into pieces.

Belcarra Regional Park on Indian Arm's southeast shore is a 240-hectare park operated by the Greater Vancouver Regional District since 1971. It includes Belcarra Peninsula and areas extending onto the mainland. It has over 9 km of marine shoreline and beaches for easy landing. Within the park there are residential areas bordering the water opposite Deep Cove (Whiskey Cove and Cozy Cove) and the west side of Bedwell Bay (Woodhaven), as well as the villages of Belcarra and Anmore and the city of Port Moody. Three archaeological sites dating back 3,000 years have been identified in the park and over 1,700 artifacts have been found.

The Belcarra picnic area (opposite Boulder Island) was once the main winter village for the Tseil-Waututh people. It is an excellent spot to combine an intertidal walk with your kayaking. There are numerous plants and creatures, including crabs, sea stars (purple, leather and sunflower), limpets, barnacles and mussels. Attached to wharf pilings are lemon nudibranches and Obelia sp., a relative of the sea anemone that looks like a plant but is an animal. Seals, raccoons, eagles, double crested cormorants, osprey, herons and kingfishers may be seen on the beaches and in the water.

There is a white house on the grounds to the south of the park picnic area. It is the house of the son of Judge Bole, who defended John Hall, the original owner of Turtlehead and Whiskey Cove and over half of the Belcarra Peninsula, against a murder charge. Bole received all the land in exchange for defending Hall and negotiating a sentence for manslaughter instead. Judge Bole was not entirely self-serving, since he is reported to have sold some of the land and saved the money for Hall's use when released from prison. The house, called Starlight Lodge, may be restored as a heritage house.

To the south of the Bole house there is another house, 25 m up in a Douglas fir tree. In 1972 George Dyson did what every boy dreams of. He lived in this self-constructed, six-foot square, one room tree house, read a library full of sea captains' journals and researched and built baidarkas, the kayaks used by the Aleuts for fishing and hunting off the coast of Alaska. During his time in the Belcarra area he constructed numerous baidarkas, most of them 4.5, 8.5 and 9.5 m long for one to three

paddlers. In 1975 he built the *Mount Fairweather*, a baidarka to surpass all others, which was 14.6 m in length and held six paddlers.

While travelling in his own handmade baidarka along the British Columbia coast Dyson developed an appreciation for the beauty, solitude and energy of the West Coast. He is described by some as a "historian among futurists." Despite (or perhaps because of) never having completed any formal education beyond age 17, Dyson is a well-respected researcher and author of the books *Baidarka the Kayak* and more recently *Darwin Among the Machines: The Evolution of Global Intelligence* and *Project Orion: The True Story of the Atomic Spaceship.*

Paddle past the Belcarra Park wharf into Belcarra Bay. On the Turtlehead side of the Bay, see if you can find any remaining rock terraces and walls, built by the hermit "Jonesy" in the 1950s as he attempted to tidy up the seashore. Now head to the privately owned Hamber Island which is opposite Turtlehead Point (look at the map—it really does look like a turtle). The inviting sand beaches on either side of the passage between the island and the mainland are private. The island was named after Eric Hamber, who in 1922 was Lieutenant Governor of B.C. and owned the island. The sand stretches across the bottom in this area, giving a very white look to the water.

In the Whiskey Cove area there is one little old cottage, built in 1909 by architect T.E. Julian, that has been left in its original design, while above it large mansions cling to the cliffs.

Some of George Dyson's creations can still be found in the Belcarra woods.

The name of the cove is said to have originated during Prohibition, when rum-runners kept their boats here. In this area look for the amazing metal elevator that stops at the guest house and extends to the dock, and for the solar panels on the West-Coast-design house close to the cottage.

Cozy Cove is the last small area of houses along the coast. It is also the last remaining area of Belcarra that is accessible only by boat or by the Jug Island Trail.

Round the point, and Jug Island beach is on the peninsula and can provide a place for a stretch before heading back to Deep Cove.

The Owl and the Pussy-Cat went to sea
In a beautiful pea-green boat.

from The Owl and the Pussy-Cat,
by Edward Lear (1812–1888)

6 Deep Cove to Bedwell Bay, Twin Islands and Thwaytes Landing

Difficulty Beginner conditions – low risk

Distances 2.5 nmi to the end of Bedwell Bay
2.65 nmi direct to Twin Islands or 3 nmi via Jug Island
1.6 nmi from Twin Islands to Thwaytes Landing
4.0 nmi from Thwaytes landing back to Deep Cove
8.5 nmi total for round trip via Jug Island to Twin islands and on to Thwaytes Landing

Duration 3–4 hours round trip

Charts 3311 Sunshine Coast—Vancouver Harbour to Desolation Sound, 1:40,000
3494 Vancouver Harbour, Central Portion, 1:10,000;
Second Narrows, 1:6,000
3495 Vancouver Harbour, Eastern Portion, 1:10,000;
Indian Arm, 1:30,000

Launching and take-out sites

The best launch site is from the beach in Deep Cove, immediately beside the Deep Cove Canoe and Kayak rental location. Their building also contains change facilities and washrooms. Access is easy and there are plenty of amenities nearby to have a bite to eat before or after your paddle. It is also possible to launch at both Cates Park and Barnet Marine Parks.

Getting there

Deep Cove is accessed from either Mount Seymour Parkway or the Dollarton Highway. Exit east from Highway 1 to either of these roads. Follow Mount Seymour Parkway for about 5.5 km or Dollarton Highway for about 7 km until their junction with Deep Cove Road. The landmark Raven Pub is a few buildings in from the corner and is a great place for an après paddle drink. Follow Deep Cove Road north for 1.2 km until the road swings right and turns into Gallant Road. Go to the end of Gallant Road and turn right. About 100 m along on the left of Banbury Road is the public access to Deep Cove. There is loading area right beside the beach.

Cates Park is accessed directly from the Dollarton Highway, about 6 km east of Highway #1.

Barnet Marine Park is located south of the Barnet Highway on the south side of Burnaby Mountain. From Burnaby take Hastings Street east until it turns into the Barnet Highway. Follow the signs to the park.

Parking

Deep Cove—There is plenty of free parking in lots parallel to Rockcliff Street to the south of Deep Cove and in Panorama Park on Panorama Drive, directly behind the cove. Overnight parking is not permitted, however. If you end up parking on the street, be aware of local parking restrictions.
Cates Park—in parking lot.
Barnet Park—in parking lot.

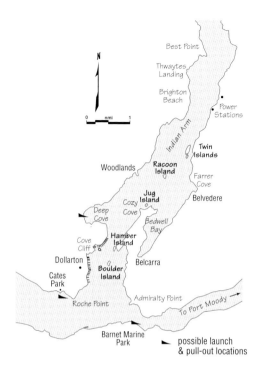

N

0   nmi   1

Best Point

Thwaytes Landing

Brighton Beach

Power Stations

Indian Arm

Twin Islands

Woodlands

Racoon Island

Farrer Cove

Jug Island

Belvedere

Cozy Cove

Deep Cove

Bedwell Bay

Cove Cliff

Hamber Island

Dollarton

Boulder Island

Belcarra

Cates Park

Admiralty Point

To Port Moody

Roche Point

Barnet Marine Park

➤ possible launch & pull-out locations

Washrooms

There are washrooms and change rooms in the Deep Cove Canoe and Kayak building in Deep Cove and in Panorama Park to the north of the Deep Cove launch site, Cates Park, Barnet Park, Belcarra Park main park area, Maple Beach and Jug Island Beach (opposite Jug Island).

Paddling considerations

Heavy motorized boat traffic in the summer. Traffic is heaviest on weekends, especially near the Deep Cove Marina on the north side of Deep Cove and in the middle of Indian Arm. On warm summer days a pre-dictable anabatic (inflow) wind blows from the south up Indian arm starting at around 11:00 am. Keep this in mind as you paddle north. The return trip may be a lot more challenging than expected, and the winds will not die down again until the evening. In the colder months, the opposite can occur, with a strong outflow wind blowing from the north and whipping up stormy conditions.

The route

Before you leave the Cove, look at the town landscape in front of you. Where restaurants, shops and cafés now stand, there used to be buildings that represented a much simpler way of life and pleasures.

Where the Seacove Marina is presently located there was a limestone quarry. From the late 1920s until the mid-1940s, directly above the government wharf, there was a dance hall called the Deep Cove Resort. The scene of many budding romances, it also gained a reputation for the Saturday night dance being a wild event. Despite this, or because of it, locals, campers and Vancouverites arrived by ferry, foot, canoe or car to dance to an orchestra until midnight. A roller rink was added beside the dance hall to make a real entertainment complex.

After the Second World War the lots where the dance hall had stood were sold for housing. The Deep Cove Canoe and Kayak rentals cement shop used to be the boathouse for the rental boats of the Deep Cove Motel, which was immediately above the area. Previously it had operated for three years as a boys camp with six log cabins.

Begin your paddle by heading across the inlet to Jug Island, part of Belcarra Regional Park. This island used to have a "handle" of rock and dirt but in the mid-1800s the handle fell into the sea. Across from the island there is a gravel beach where it's possible to have a rest, snack or washroom break early in your trip.

As you paddle around Seal Rock at the point of the peninsula, you will enter Bedwell Bay. This bay was named after the second ship's master by Captain George Richards of the Royal Navy when he was mapping the area between 1857 and 1860. It will take about an hour to paddle to the end of the bay and back from Jug Island. Belcarra Regional Park lies on either side of the bay, although interspersed with residential areas on the east side.

After the Second World War, Bedwell Bay was used as an anchorage and storage for retired naval ships and minesweepers. It also became the graveyard for a number of abandoned boats. A mystery wreck was identified here in 1994 by the Underwater Archaeological Society of B.C. Based on research and drawings of the remains, it was believed to be a sealing schooner sunk at some time after legislation ended the seal trade in 1911. As well, there is a minesweeper and a 34-metre fish-packing vessel that in the 1970s was a rehabilitation home for wayward teens (which mysteriously burned one weekend just after they left the boat). All of this metal beneath you makes for excellent wreck diving and fishing in the area.

After paddling to the end of Bedwell Bay and back (or not, depending on your choices) you will pass by an area that was called Woodhaven. The trees in this area were all logged by 1905 and no wonder! Some were 2.4 m in diameter and provided seemingly endless resources for lumber and shingles. By 1910, subdivision of the land had started and summer homes began to be built.

You will pass by the area called Belvedere, meaning "beautiful view," and then past Farrer Cove, which is one of the residential areas opposite Jug Island and was named after the first landowner, George Farrer. He had an orchard that helped provide fruit to the residents along the Arm. Locally grown food such as his was picked up by a small "store boat" and homeowners got dockside purchase and delivery.

In 1947 the YMCA built Camp Howdy in this area and operated it as a camp for children. However, in 2004 the Y entered discussions with the Village of Belcarra and the Greater Vancouver Regional District to sell and develop the property as residential housing in order to finance and update their other camps and programs.

Head past Indian Point for Twin Islands, which will be about another half-hour paddle. Indian Point was named in recognition of the heroic efforts made by an Indian mother to save her three children after her canoe upset. Unfortunately the baby of the three toddlers drowned.

On your way to Twin Islands you will pass by Raccoon Island. The Twin Islands and Raccoon Island are part of Indian Arm Marine Provincial Park. At low tide there is a landing on the northern shore of Raccoon, and swimming and scuba diving is good in the vicinity of the island. If you look around on the island, you will see holes left from an exploration for blue diamonds that were rumoured to be there. Blue diamonds are among the world's rarest (the Hope diamond, now in the Smithsonian Institution in Washington, D.C., was the biggest at 112 3/16 carats). It is said that a large proportion of present-day British Columbians are counting on the lottery for their retirement plan, so hunting for these blue diamonds was perhaps an early variation on the hope of easy riches.

The Twin Islands consist of Big Twin and Little Twin. These islands were once a centrally located food-gathering spot for the Tsleil-Waututh (Burrard) First Nations. In the early 1900s the islands were subdivided into 17 lots to be developed as a summer resort, and some cottages were constructed on them. By the 1940s they once again became isolated enough for a hermit to live on one of the islands. On the eastern shore, opposite Twin Islands, a Swedish entrepreneur in the late 1950s set up a sawmill using logs left after logging to make cedar planks for caskets.

At low tide you can walk between the two islands and there is an easy landing, but keep an eye on an incoming tide or watch your kayak float away. When there is enough water to paddle between the two islands there is still a good landing, with some gravel, on the east side of Little Twin. Camping is allowed and wooden tent platforms are provided on Big Twin. There is also a dock and an outhouse on the east side of Big Twin.

In the distance, you can see part of the Buntzen Hydro Plant. This part is the southern power station, No. 2, built in 1914. The original part of the plant, Buntzen Power Plant No. 1, can be seen as you progress further north. It was built in 1903–04 and used water from Buntzen Lake directly above it (also called Lake Beautiful at the time) and from Lake Coquitlam, with the water coming through a 3.6-km tunnel to Buntzen Lake. The solid concrete building sits on a ledge that was blasted from the rock. From 1930 to the 1950s there was a community with homes and a school for the children of the plant workers. A wooden boardwalk connected the two facilities. These were all demolished when the plant was switched to automatic controls and workers were no longer needed to run it. The plant continues to operate by remote control from Vancouver and provides power to Ioco in Port Moody and the oil facilities in Burnaby, as well as additional electricity when needed to a substation in Burnaby.

Paddle across the Arm, over to the west shore and Brighton Beach. The low buildings with orange roofs are the Camp Jubilee Retreat and Conference Centre. This property was owned by John Rainey, who lived a secluded life here while he mined the area for gold and silver. Upon his death the land was sold, with plans for facilities for veterans' families. Another southern portion of the land was turned into Camp Jubilee in the 1930s by the women of the Workers Unity League as a camp for children and parents who were on social assistance. Today it is run by the Indian Arm Recreational Services as a summer camp for children 7 to 17 and a retreat/conference centre.

In the same area, slightly to the north, is the 62.5-hectare property of Thwaytes Landing, named after Captain Thwaytes, who in the 1930s cleared a large portion of the land and used the waterfalls to provide electric light. He had a poultry farm that supplied eggs for people along the Arm. The white house perched on the cliff was built in 1927 as a summer home for the Underhill family and will be part of the facilities of a proposed day-use park created from the Thwaytes property. Funding is presently being raised through a yearly paddle-a-thon

and other events sponsored by the Land Conservancy to pay off their portion of the land cost. The land is already secured with payments by the District of North Vancouver and the Greater Vancouver Regional District. This is a good spot to land and have lunch or take a walk to the falls. Take time to read the messages carved into the logs around the property by its previous owner, Mearnie Summer, who sold the property to the three organizations for far less than a developer would have paid, so it could remain in a natural state.

You have now paddled about halfway up the inlet. Lion's Nose (officially known as Best Point) is at the narrowest part of Indian Arm. A legend is told that a sea serpent got stuck between the cliffs with its head on the west shore and its tail on the east shore. The superstition that death came to those who went between the cliffs meant that many native people portaged this area.

At the most northerly end of the inlet (an overnight trip for most kayakers) is the Wigwam Inn. It was opened in 1910 and enjoyed fame with guests such as John D. Rockefeller paying $3.50 a day to stay, wander along wild trails and enjoy the Spray of Pearls waterfall. The initial plan had included a development of a summer resort called Indian River Park, with sale of lots around the Inn to individuals. The investor planned to use Indian names for the street names, which is how the name Wigwam Inn originated. It was operated with varying success until 1962 when a casino operating on the premises was raided by the RCMP. Despite other

An early "Tuesday night" Deep Cove race, with canoes instead of kayaks.
Photo courtesy Deep Cove Heritage Society.

attempts to restore the premises, it was not until 1986, when the Royal Vancouver Yacht Club bought it as an outstation, that it was restored to its former glory.

Opposite Raccoon Island on the western shore are the two residential areas of Sunshine (to the north) and Woodlands. In the early days of settlement, they were separated by a large cliff and connected by a path. Both of these areas were primarily summer resorts and originally only accessible by the various boats that ferried people to and fro for summer fun. This remoteness is reported to have suited the mothers of daughters very well since it meant that their girls weren't easily able to go dancing at the Deep Cove dance hall. Instead they had to be content with the entertainment of swimming and regattas unless they had the 50 cents to pay someone to row them to town. The Indian River Road was eventually extended to these two areas for easier access, although residents continue to pay for maintenance of the suicidally steep and incredibly twisty road.

There are several interesting homes in this area, one of them being on a small island with a cement bridge going to it. This island was transformed into a garden surrounding the house called Samarkand ("Heart's Desire") with walkways, trellises and flowers and shrubs. Some of the remnants of a seawall can be seen. The present house was used for parts of the filming of the Disney-produced TV series Danger Bay, which ran from 1984 to 1990. Another home is one that has a Chinese-appearing pagoda on the one side. It was built in the early 1900s for the Ward family and today still looks very similar to original pictures.

Mount Seymour Provincial Park features Mount Seymour, which towers 1455 m above the south end of Indian Arm. There are numerous hiking trails and downhill and cross-country ski areas.

As you re-enter Deep Cove, high above you on the right on a rocky outcropping you can usually see hikers looking down at you. They are on part of the Baden-Powell Trail that goes from Deep Cove to Horseshoe Bay. This trail was built by boy scouts to honour the founder of the scouting movement, Lord Baden-Powell. Each year in July, an ultramarathon, the Knee Knackering North Shore Trail Run, is held on this 50-km trail across three local mountains. In 2004 the winning time was 5:02:21. What madness when they could be kayaking!

Where now a luxurious private home sits at the end of Panorama Drive below the Lookout rock, in the early 1900s the Quarries Lodge offered summer accommodation. During the war years it had difficulty getting supplies and gradually ceased hotel business. In the early 1950s it collapsed into the sea and the remains had to be dragged up and towed to shore. A marina was expanded in the waterfront area of the former lodge.

Although you can't see it, another trail, this one stretching some 80 km all the way around Indian Arm from Elsay Peak in Mount Seymour Park to the Dilly-Dally trail at Buntzen Lake, has recently been completed by Don McPherson. He is one of the two mountaineers who constructed the Grouse Grind 20 years ago. While the sections of the Baden-Powell trail can be done by recreational hikers, McPherson cautions that the Indian Arm route is for those with "a high degree of fitness and some mountaineering skills." Much of the trail is on land now co-managed by the Tsleil-Waututh people and BC Parks. BC Parks has expressed concern about degradation of the watershed and about accidents in terrain where rescue is difficult.

Back to the beach and a reward of ice-cream, a latte or a more substantial meal in the cafés and restaurants of Deep Cove that continue to maintain the same holiday atmosphere they have had for over 80 years.

For she is such a smart little craft,
Such a neat little, sweet little craft,
Such a bright little,
Tight little,
Slight little,
Light little,
Trim little, slim little craft!

from Gilbert & Sullivan's Ruddigore,
lyric by Sir William Schwenk Gilbert (1836–1911)

7 Ambleside to Point Atkinson, Lighthouse Park

Difficulty Intermediate conditions – moderate risk

Distance 9 nmi round trip

Duration 3–4 hours round trip

Charts 3311 Sunshine Coast—Vancouver Harbour to Desolation Sound, 1:40,000
3463 Strait of Georgia, Southern Portion, 1:80,000
3481 Approaches to Vancouver Harbour, 1:25,000
3493 Vancouver Harbour, Western Portion, 1:10,000

Launching and take-out sites

You can launch either from the beach in front of Ambleside Park or from the beach beside the cement ramp west of the Hollyburn Yacht Club.

An alternative launch site for a shorter trip is at West Bay Park.

Getting there

From Vancouver, cross the Lions Gate Bridge and exit at the north end onto Marine Drive heading west. Continue along Marine Drive past Park Royal Mall. Turn south onto 13th Street. Cross the rail line to reach Ambleside Park and Hollyburn Yacht Club.

If you are launching at West Bay Park, continue driving along Marine Drive past Dundarave. After you pass 31st Street and go under a railway bridge, turn south onto Radcliffe Avenue. Continue west to the end of the road and Maple Lane.

From elsewhere in the Lower Mainland, take Highway #1 and exit south at Taylor Way. Follow Taylor Way to the bottom of the steep hill, then turn west on Marine Drive and follow the instructions above.

Parking

Parking is free at Ambleside Park. There is limited three-hour parking on Radcliffe Avenue above West Bay Park. A municipal sign in the area asks park visitors to park their vehicles on Marine Drive.

Washrooms

Public washrooms are available at Ambleside Park, Dundarave Park and West Bay Park.

Paddling considerations

The West Vancouver waterfront is fairly exposed to the west and south. Strong winds and large waves can come from both directions. There is a noticeable current near the mouth of the Capilano River and the Lions Gate Bridge. Steep waves will develop when an ebb (outgoing) tide meets waves in English Bay. Cross-chop and rebounding waves are common off Point Atkinson.

The route

The Hollyburn Sailing Club, beside which you may launch your kayak, was founded in 1963 with 20 members. It is a volunteer organization that offers recreational and racing opportunities for all ages and levels of sailors.

Guide **continues on p. 99**

Lions Gate Bridge under construction, 1937–38, with the Empress of Japan II passing beneath. Photo courtesy Vancouver Public Library.

A SHORT BUT RICH HISTORY OF WEST VANCOUVER

Long before settlers claimed land along the shores of West Vancouver, the Squamish Nation used the beaches for fishing and summer living sites. José Maria Narvaez was the first recorded European to see this area, in 1791. Toward the east end of the Ambleside Seawalk, a cairn marks this event. The shoreline was accurately surveyed by Captain George Richards of the Royal Navy in 1858 when he was looking for suitable military campsites in case of a U.S. invasion.

History continues on p. 100

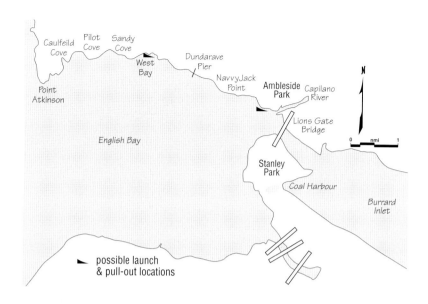

Caulfeild Cove · Pilot Cove · Sandy Cove · West Bay · Dundarave Pier · NavvyJack Point · Point Atkinson · Ambleside Park · Capilano River · Lions Gate Bridge · English Bay · Stanley Park · Coal Harbour · Burrard Inlet

N

0 nmi 1

possible launch & pull-out locations

As you are launching your boat, look southeast and you can see the green outline of Stanley Park, connected to North Vancouver by the Lions Gate Bridge. Construction of this bridge began in 1937 and was finished in 1938 at a cost of $6 million. Initially it was a toll bridge, but tolls were removed in 1963 when the Province of British Columbia bought the bridge. During construction citizens expressed concern about the building of the approach causeway through the park, just as they did when the approach was widened and the bridge refurbished from 1999 to 2002. In the course of the renovation, all 51 sections of the bridge deck, which is 80 m above the water at its highest point, were replaced. Between 60,000 and 70,000 cars a day cross the bridge. Original financing for the bridge was by the Irish brewing company Guinness, which wanted to encourage development on the North Shore. They purchased 1,619 hectares (later developed by British Pacific Properties) for $75,000 and promised a million dollars worth of improvements. The land high on the side of the mountain to the west of the bridge became known as the British Properties. It was, and still is, considered a very exclusive residential area. Until after the Second World War, there was unspoken discrimination against non-whites and non-Christians who may have wanted to purchase land.

Two carved stone lions guard the south end of the bridge, but the bridge was named not for them but for the

Guide continues on p. 101

The District of West Vancouver begins at the Capilano River, west of the Lion's Gate Bridge, and reaches westward to Howe Sound and Horseshoe Bay. West Vancouver was originally part of the District of North Vancouver until 1912 when it became incorporated as a municipality in its own right.

In the 1800s settlement concentrated on the south shore close to Granville (Vancouver) and Moodyville (east of the Lions Gate Bridge) in North Vancouver. Lumbering provided giant cedars and firs to the sawmills that were established in these areas. By 1867 there were two mills east of the First Narrows, and individuals were beginning to look at the slopes of West Vancouver for new timber resources. Logging camps and a fish cannery were established along the shores of Ambleside and Dundarave, and extensive logging occurred in the Hollyburn region. By the early 1900s there were a few homes and many visitors who would camp along the shores in the summer for their wilderness holiday experience. Once ferry transportation was established, increased settlement and development of businesses to support the new population began. From a modest beginning, primarily based on the lumber industry, West Vancouver never looked back. Although it now has no heavy industry as part of its economic base, it lays claim to being the municipality with the highest per capita income in Canada.

❧

twin mountain peaks that tower over the North Shore, which are called The Lions.

The lights on the bridge, when seen from a distance, create a jewel necklace across the water at night. They were donated by the Guinness family at the time of Vancouver's Expo 86.

Slightly to the west of the Lions Gate Bridge, in Stanley Park, is Prospect Point, where a lighthouse was built at sea level in 1898, ten years after the SS *Beaver*, the first and most famous steamship to work along the West Coast, ran aground at "Calamity Point" (Prospect Point). Eventually the hulk slipped off the rocks and sank, but it makes a ghostly reappearance at very low tides when the frame of it can still be seen. In 1909 terraces and a signal station were built to direct the increasing number of ships into Burrard Inlet and Harbour. These terraces now serve as a lookout to the North Shore and beyond, for the numerous tourists who visit the park.

On the north shore at the mouth of the Capilano River, the Capilano Fog and Light Station was built. Along with the Prospect Point lighthouse, it was constructed to alert ships that they were approaching the narrowest and most treacherous part of the inlet. In 1915 the lighthouse and the keeper's house were built on stilts, and so were nearly always surrounded by water. By 1925 wood worms and seawater had deteriorated the wooden structure, but there continued to be a light keeper in residence until 1946. Today, an automated beacon on a concrete base replaces the original structure, which was deliberately demolished by fire in 1969.

Looking east on the North Shore, you will see the beginning of Ambleside Park. It was designated as a park in 1918. The east side of the park is

Ambleside Beach east of 14th Street, ca. 1918. Photo courtesy West Vancouver Museum & Archives.

owned by Squamish First Nations. There is a welcoming totem on the spit of land, as well as a plaque showing First Nations people in a canoe with Stanley Park in the background. The picture depicts the Squamish Nation's long association with this area, which they named Swaywi. The First Nations are presently planning a development that may see more high-rise buildings constructed north and east of the park on their reserve land.

The English name Ambleside was given in memory of an early resident's English hometown. To the east of Ambleside there was a large lagoon and marsh used as a booming grounds from about 1870 to 1890. The present lagoon is the result of sawdust and sawmill waste being dumped into the area as fill, leaving only the small duck pond as open water.

Although there had always been some sort of marine transportation (sailboats, rowboats, canoes) to access settlements along the North Shore, it was not until 1909 that ferry service began to West Vancouver, initiated by John Lawson. He used his boats to bring real estate investors over to preview property. The new city of West Vancouver took over the service from the West Vancouver Transportation Company and in 1912 ran the West Van No. 1 from downtown Vancouver to a dock at Ambleside. The trip took about 25 minutes, and the vessels used the slogan "first ferry to the new city." These ferries also took day trippers to places such as Horseshoe Bay. A ferry building was constructed and now serves as an art gallery, found a little to the west of the launch site, facing the roadway.

Navvy Jack Point, the waterfront area between 19th and 20th Streets, ca. 1927. Photo courtesy West Vancouver Museum & Archives.

Multi-million dollar homes line the West Vancouver waterfront.

Navvy Jack Point is west of John Lawson Park between 20th and 22nd Streets. It is named after the Welshman John Thomas, who operated the first ferry in Burrard Inlet between Brighton (east of Granville/Vancouver) and Moodyville (east of the present Lions Gate Bridge) and Stamp's sawmills. In 1874, after a competitor started a similar ferry route and put him out of business, Navvy Jack Thomas purchased land in the area of 16th Avenue and started a gravel supply business using gravel from the mouth of the Capilano River. Later he subdivided and sold the property. John Lawson—for whom Lawson Park, situated along the waterfront is named—bought the property in 1906 and lived there for many years.

Paddle along the waterfront where the Centennial Seawalk runs from Ambleside to Dundarave. In the 1920s small beach houses, serving as vacation homes for Vancouverites, lined the waterfront. Now, towering apartment buildings look out to ever-changing views of Burrard Inlet.

The farther west you paddle, the more this trip becomes a real-estate viewing trip. Luxurious houses line the shore, with designs and styles of every description.

The next point of interest is Dundarave Park and Pier. The area gets its name from Dundarave Castle in Loch Fine in Scotland. The pier was built in 1914 to accommodate ferry traffic from downtown Vancouver. This service was supplanted by John Lawson's ferries, since the pier itself was too exposed to waves and weather for easy landings. However, it became a site of regattas, swimming in a pool constructed to the east of it and an outdoor extension for the social activities held at the nearby Clachan restaurant and hotel. The restaurant, whose name is Gaelic for "meeting place," was built in 1912 by two sisters, Jessie and Nellie Stevenson. Having undergone structural changes and changed hands numerous times over the years, the place is now a heritage site operated by local owners as the popular Beach House Restaurant.

Between the pier and West Bay, keep your eyes alert at low tide for an urban sea cave. Built of concrete to house and launch a speedboat, it looks like a set from a James Bond movie. In fact, with the luxury houses, the train, the fast boats, possibly a hidden helicopter pad to make an escape, this whole area could be a movie set!

Continue along to Altamont Beach Park, where there is another small stretching place on your way to West Bay. West Bay Park is identifiable by the concrete wall and park benches on a grassy level area with a bubbling steam running down the west side of the park into the ocean. The Squamish name for West Bay was Smelakwa, and it was noted as a source of Alaska blueberries.

After leaving West Bay, go close to the shore and look at several of the houses. The one at the point as you

Dundarave Park, the original Clachan Hotel and pier, ca. 1918. Photo courtesy West Vancouver Memorial Library.

Caulfeild Cove wharf, West Vancouver, with SS Britannia, ca. 1910–15.
Photo courtesy West Vancouver Memorial Library.

leave the bay follows the contours of the point both in its main form and in the roof and overhang details. Around the corner is a masterpiece of cement stonework that duplicates an unbroken sheet of stone with greenery at different levels. It looks perfectly natural until you realize that it is highly unlikely that horizontal trenches would be that symmetrical.

As you paddle along you may hear the chug and whistle of a passing train. This is the Canadian National that just left its yard in North Vancouver and is heading to Prince George. This rail line was incorporated in 1912 as the Pacific Great Eastern Railway to replace the Howe Sound & Northern Railway. A line was completed in 1914 (although not used between 1928 and 1956) to run from North Vancouver to Whytecliff (south of Horseshoe Bay). A line between Squamish

and Prince George was completed in 1952. The "missing link" between North Vancouver and Squamish was completed in 1956. The railway has been renamed several times: it became British Columbia Rail in 1972 and BC Rail in 1984. A provincial government initiative resulted in the railway merging with CN Rail in July 2004. The line presently carries only freight, except for a shuttle train between Lillooet and Darcy. A historic steam train, the Royal Hudson #2860, ran as a day excursion to Squamish for 25 years until 2000. It was withdrawn from service because the government decided not to support the program and the train needed a costly refit. Luckily, the West Coast Railway Association developed a proposal that will see the train returned to specialized service in 2005, so once again you may hear and see it as you paddle along. It is also proposed to use the train for both promotional trips and special train service during the 2010 Olympic year.

Following along the curves of the shore you will come to Sandy Cove, where the Great Northern Cannery stood from 1891 until 1967. Environment Canada's Pacific Research Laboratories are now located on this spot.

Pilot Cove, which is around the next curving point, was named for the ship pilots who lived in a house that was built by Francis William Caulfeild. These pilots helped guide the schooners and other large vessels through the First Narrows on their way to or from the Vancouver docks. During the day, a flag on a tall pole indicated whether a pilot was available, and at night a coal-oil lamp indicated the pilothouse location.

The original 1874 Point Atkinson Lighthouse, ca. 1909. Photo courtesy West Vancouver Museum & Archives.

The next cove is Caulfeild Cove, named after the same man who built the pilothouse and proceeded to develop his own village following the contoured and rocky landscape of the land he had purchased. Consequently, the narrow roads nearby, with English names such as Piccadilly and Clovelly Walk, often twist and turn. Caulfeild donated land for a village green and established a post office and general store to provide for the "villagers," who often were influential citizens from Vancouver.

Also at Caulfeild Cove, formerly called Skunk Cove, Caulfeild built a dock that was big enough to handle the steamers run by the Harbour Navigation.

The waterfront, from Pilot Cove around to Lighthouse Park, was preserved as parkland by Caulfeild. Depending on the weather and wave action at Point Atkinson, you could pull out for a rest at the beach or at the district dock in Caulfeild Cove.

Point Atkinson, named by Captain Vancouver for a friend, and Lighthouse Park are the turnaround point of this trip. The First Nations name for the point was Skay-witsut. The first wooden lighthouse here was built in 1874. The present one was built in 1912 and switched to automatic controls in 1996.

The lighthouse keepers at Point Atkinson initially were isolated from everyone except those who arrived by sea. Eventually Marine Drive was extended and an access road to the lighthouse was built. Now, 10 km of trails wind through the surrounding park and down to the lighthouse.

You can see one gun tower on the east side of the lighthouse. It was built during the Second World War, as were the towers across English Bay at Point Grey, to serve for early warning and defence outposts.

When returning to the launch site, you may want to head directly back rather than paddle into all the coves again.

You may pass by freighters waiting to enter the Port of Vancouver, and see cruise ships entering or leaving. Look under the Lions Gate Bridge and you are looking in the direction of a major contributor to Vancouver's economy. The Port of Vancouver transits $29 billion in goods annually and contributes $3.5 billion to Canada's gross domestic product. It extends for 233 km of coastline, from Roberts Bank at the Canada/U.S. border, along the north and south shores of Burrard Inlet and up Indian Arm. It handles 60–70 million tonnes of cargo from 90 different world economies. There are 17 bulk terminals, three break bulk terminals and two cruise terminals.

What is in all those ships? From May to September, 300 sailings leave the cruise terminal carrying nearly one million revenue passengers. The bulk carriers transport coal, grain, sulphur, potash, liquid chemicals and specialty grain products. The break bulk ships transport lumber, wood and other value-added cargo.

By taking a straight route back to Ambleside, even if you have to detour around a large anchored bulk carrier, you will decrease your return time and allow yourself time for a wander through the Ferry Building Art Gallery or along the village streets of

The prosperity of the port city is apparent in this West Vancouver residential real estate near West Bay.

Passengers disembarking from SS Britannia *at Snug Cove, Bowen Island, the "Happy Isle." Photo courtesy Vancouver Public Library.*

A CIRCULAR HISTORY
OF BOWEN ISLAND

BOWEN ISLAND, like the majority of the islands in and near the Strait of Georgia, was the home of First Nations peoples for thousands of years. It was also a place for inter-tribal meetings among coastal peoples. The island was named Xwlil-xhwm, meaning "fast drumming ground," perhaps because of the drumming that may have occurred during these meetings. Each part of the Island had its own Salish name, such as Qole'laqom, which was probably a summer campsite; Naych-chail-kun, meaning "outside of the islands," for the south coast; and Kwumch-nam, meaning "noise as when stamping heels," for Hood Point.

History continues on p. 108

8 Snug Cove to Mount Gardner Bay or Bowen Bay

Difficulty Intermediate conditions – moderate risk

Distances 7 nmi to Mount Gardner Bay
3.5 nmi from Mount Gardner Bay to Bowen Bay

Durations 3 hours to Mount Gardner Bay
5 hours to Bowen Bay one way

Charts 3311 Sunshine Coast – Vancouver Harbour to Desolation Sound, 1:40,000
3512 Strait of Georgia Central Portion, 1:80,000
3526 Howe Sound, 1:40,000

Launch site
Snug Cove to the west of the marina along Lady Alexandra Promenade.

Take-out site
Mount Gardner Bay or Bowen Bay on the west side of Bowen Island.

Getting there
Bowen Island is a scenic 20-minute ferry ride from the Horseshoe Bay ferry terminal, located on the west side of Vancouver's North Shore. To get to the ferry terminal, take the Upper Levels/Highway 1 west from anywhere in the Lower Mainland.

Guide **continues on p. 111**

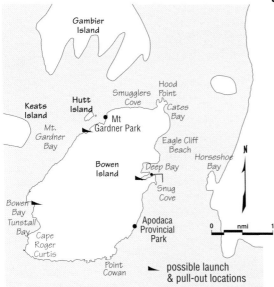

possible launch & pull-out locations

Bowen was first charted in 1791, by the Spanish Captain Narvaez, who called it Isla de Apodaca after a Spanish military leader and administrator. Captain Vancouver sailed in the area the next year and named Howe Sound after an English military leader but did not land on the island or name it.

In 1860 Captain Richards charted much of the surrounding waters and renamed the island after a British naval officer, Admiral James Bowen, who had helped defeat the French fleet in 1794 under the leadership of Admiral Howe. Many of the other place names on Bowen Island, such as Grafton Bay and Dorman Bay, were given in recognition of the contributions made by early settlers to the development of Bowen Island.

Initially, logging provided work on the Island. In addition to sending raw logs to the mills in False Creek,

History **continues on p. 112**

Picnic grounds on Deep Bay, Bowen Island, ca. 1915–20. Photo courtesy Vancouver Public Library.

A BC Ferry dominates the Snug Cove waterfront.

You can either drive onto the ferry or park your car in the BC Ferries parking lot and walk aboard. Walking aboard is the recommended method if you are renting boats or have kayak transport wheels to cart your own craft. Follow the passenger drop-off and parking lot signs as you approach the ferry terminal. If you are driving aboard, signs will direct you to the dedicated payment booth for the Bowen Island ferry. Arriving early will ensure you do not get left behind. Although the ferry runs often, on busy summer weekends cars do get left behind. Call 1-888-BC-FERRY or surf to www.bcferries.com for schedule and fare information.

Parking

The parking in Horseshoe Bay has been pretty much monopolized by BC Ferries. All nearby streets are signed to prevent parking for more than an hour or two, so save yourself the stress of finding a free spot and plan on paying if you are parking in Horseshoe Bay. On Bowen Island there is pay parking close to the marina and free parking on nearby streets.

Washrooms

The Union Steamship Company marina in Snug Cove has washrooms and also a pay shower. Bowen Island Sea Kayak has change rooms.

Guide continues on p. 113

sawmills and a shingle operations sprang up on Bowen. Whaling boats were moored in the harbours and whales caught among the surrounding islands. The first Bowen resident, in the 1870s, was a logger, and was soon followed by other settlers who were fishermen, farmers, copper miners and labourers in a brick works and a dynamite factory.

The dynamite factory was started in 1908 at Tunstall Bay, on the southwest shore, only to be moved in 1913 to James Island, off Nanaimo. Employment in the dynamite plant was probably not the first choice for Bowen Islanders, since there were numerous fatalities among its employees during only four years of operation at Tunstall Bay. Many of the workers were Chinese and Japanese who had limited English and are presumed to have had trouble reading safety precautions related to handling the dynamite.

The history of Bowen Island is inextricably linked with boats and, with the boats, tourism. Early on, in

History continues on p. 114

Small craft in Snug Cove, Bowen Island, ca. 1913. Photo courtesy City of Vancouver Archives.

Paddling considerations

Watch for ferries and pleasure craft entering and leaving docks at Snug Cove. Ocean conditions, with high waves, tides and currents, can suddenly occur at any time. Watch for choppy seas near headlands, especially Hood Point. Ferries transiting to Langdale, Horseshoe Bay and Snug Cove can throw up large waves that do not get to you until well after the ship has passed.

While you may be enticed into thinking you can paddle around the entire island in a short time, its coastline covers 22 nmi (41 km) and is a full day of paddling. There is also a strong possibility that ocean conditions could dramatically change during your trip, especially if you go clockwise and are more exposed to the Strait of Georgia. Winds flowing out from Howe Sound can also contribute to rough water. However, by paddling counter-clockwise you will be somewhat more protected and have several beaches to land at or use as a turnaround point along the way, even if you do not complete the three- or five-hour one-way trips suggested here.

The route

For early settlers, as for the Bowen Island residents of today, Snug Cove was the main centre of work and business. On your way to the launch site you will pass the 240-hectare Crippen Regional Park on either side of Government Road and Snug Cove. It is named after a senior consulting engineer who owned the land before it was purchased by the Greater Vancouver Regional District (GVRD). There are trails northwest to Killarney Lake and southeast to Dorman Point. The park is located on much of the same land that was part of the resort development on Bowen Island in the 1920s.

Along Government Road, on your right you will see the Union Steamship Company store. This building, built in 1924, was restored beginning in 1984 by a co-operative endeavour between Bowen Island organizations and Greater Vancouver Regional Parks. It houses the post office, just as it did when first built, Crippen Park reception, the electoral office, two rooms for community activities, and the public library. Behind the building is the Boulevard Cottage, which is one of the Union Steamship Company cottages that has been restored and now houses an information centre.

Small stores in restored heritage buildings line the west side of the road, and in July and August there are tents with a variety of good quality crafts for sale.

The second marina on Bowen was established in 1900, on the north side of Snug Cove, close to the end of the ferry dock, where it still exists today.

As you walk farther and turn towards the launch site, you will pass the Union Steamship marina, established in 1889. Beside the marina is Doc Morgan's Inn. The building was once the home of a barber, Doc Morgan, who worked in the Vancouver Hotel but on Bowen was known for his parties and seafood feasts.

Guide continues on p. 115

1913, Captain Charles Henry Cates, one of five brothers who were master mariners, had already established the C.H. Cates Towing Company, whose tugboats worked the waters of Burrard Inlet and Howe Sound. His brother Captain John Cates owned the Terminal Steamship Company and started the first cruises to Bowen. Hundreds of people crowded on large steamships, such as the *Britannia*, built at the Cates family's boat-building enterprise in False Creek, to make the trip to the "Happy Isle." Cates had the initial idea of a resort on the island, and proceeded to build the Terminal Resort, tennis courts and other amenities to accommodate the flood of visitors. In 1920 the Union Steamship Company purchased Cates's company and expanded the business. The company contributed to the development of Bowen Island by bringing thousands of people there each year for company picnics, camp, or day or evening trips to the remote location. Union Steamship also expanded the resort, building 100 additional cottages, six picnic grounds located close to the ferry docks, and an outdoor concert stage and dance pavilion that accommodated 800—the biggest in British Columbia. The fresh-air activities and environment on Bowen (as well as in Deep Cove in North Vancouver, and West Vancouver, which were experiencing a similar influx of campers, holidayers and visitors) were a big attraction, as the air in Burrard Inlet and Vancouver was increasingly polluted by the smoke of numerous industries.

Groups as diverse as the Excelsior Laundry employees, Hudson's Bay store staff, the Vancouver Fire Department and Point Grey civic employees went to Bowen for their staff picnics. Moonlight and dance cruises also enticed Vancouverites to this far-away island.

During and after the war years, however, recreational use of the island tapered off, and by the late 1950s

History continues on p. 116

The Union Steamship Company Store in Snug Cove

Along the edge of the cove is the Lady Alexandra Promenade, named after the Union Steamship Company's SS *Lady Alexandra*, which had a capacity of 1,400 passengers and transported over a million visitors to Bowen Island between 1924 and 1953.

The Davies Heritage Orchard and Cottages, located above the marina cove, retains a small number of the apple, cherry, pear and plum trees planted by Davies in the area, and two of the more than 180 small cottages that were used as rental lodging in the 1920s. One of the cottages is currently maintained as a headquarters and information centre by the Bowen Island Heritage Association and the GVRD.

Put your kayak in and paddle north toward Deep Bay (previously called Mannion Bay and sometimes Deep Cove). Pebbly Beach and Sandy Beach in this cove are spots that have been swimming beaches since the early settlement years. This bay produced clay that was made into bricks and used in construction of such Vancouver landmarks as the City Hall. It was also a moorage for the whaling ships that hunted, and eventually eliminated, humpback whales from Howe Sound.

In the heyday of the Union Steamships cruises, this bay had a dock for boats. There was a wooden walkway

Guide **continues on p. 117**

the resort foundered as the boat excursions ended. In the '60s Bowen and many other Gulf Islands were seen as hippie hangouts. But in the '70s, as island vacation homes once again rose in favour and waterfront real estate became increasingly rare, Bowen began to lure Vancouverites and others to a quieter, slower-paced life. The Island still contributes a strong presence in the arts field, and many residents now commute or run technology-based businesses so they can enjoy the sea and scenery at home on Bowen.

The official community plan hopes to limit Bowen's population to 7,200, and although there are presently only about 3,200 permanent residents, you may want to buy now or remain a day tripper!

 භ

Bowen Island, Snug Cove and Deep Bay are as beautiful from the air as they are from the water.

that went from Snug Cove over toward the Bay. A bridge over the lagoon from where the large steamships docked in Snug Cove led to tennis courts, a bowling green and a putting green, as well as The Bowen Inn (formerly the Terminal Hotel).

You are paddling in Queen Charlotte Channel as you go north past Ecclestone Beach to Miller's Landing Beach. The majority of these beaches are the front yards of local residents, so think twice before using them as an outhouse. The third beach in this area is Eagle Cliff Beach. There is a dream house abandoned along these shores, waiting for someone to complete it in the way the new luxurious one has been constructed a little further along the route.

Cates Bay (named after the ubiquitous seagoing Cates family) and a small beach are just before Hood Point and Finisterre Island, which at low tide is connected to the mainland. A modern windmill tower is silhouetted against the sky on Finisterre and, given the prevailing winds down Howe Sound, should produce quite a bit of energy. Bowyer Island is off the mainland coast northeast of Bowen, and along the coast you can see from south to north: Black, Strachan, The Lions, Harvey and Brunswick mountains.

A historic Union Steamship Company cottage

Once you round Hood Point, to the north you can see Gambier Island.

After you pass the houses along the shore of Smugglers Cove you will see a lot of trees, rocks and a few eagles. This small cove is believed to have been a harbour for rum smugglers during U.S. Prohibition in the 1920s, although no specific reference to Bowen or this bay has ever been found in official documents.

Continue along to Grafton Bay and then to Mount Gardner Park, with its small pebbled beach which looks out onto Hutt Island. This is an excellent spot to have lunch and contemplate whether you want to go on to Bowen Bay (possibly another two hours of paddling) or pull out at Mount Gardner Bay and the Mount Gardner public dock a short way along the shore.

Whether you go on to Bowen Bay or stop here, you will need to hitchhike back to Snug Cove to pick up your car, or have an arranged pickup by friends who may have been hiking on the island. Bowen Island Taxi can also be called upon for pickup at 604-947-0000. You may also be able to arrange a pickup from Bowen Island Sea Kayak if they are operating tours in the vicinity.

It will take you about another two hours of steady paddling to get to Bowen Bay. There are no easy spots for a pullout or a rest on this portion of the trip. You have clear views of Keats Island to the west and the eight islands that make up the Pasley group to the south. These islands also make a very good kayaking day trip. As well, you may see BC Ferries on their way to and from the Langdale ferry dock on the Sunshine Coast.

The community of Bowen Bay began as a co-operative of 14 people who bought the land in 1943. If you arrive on any sunny summer afternoon you will find the water and shore filled with children and adults of all ages. It is a favourite swimming spot for Islanders and visitors alike and catches the last afternoon sun.

Load up your kayak, return to Snug Cove, and while you wait for the ferry, explore the historic buildings, have a glass of Bowen brew, walk to the fish ladders on the way to Killarney Lake or enjoy the comings and goings of people and boats on this peaceful island.

Beautiful isle of the sea,
Smile on the brow of the waters.

from Song, *by*
George Cooper (1820–1876)

9 Deas Island Slough to Wellington Point Park

Difficulty Beginner conditions – low risk

Distance 8.5 nmi round trip

Duration 3–4 hours round trip depending on how well you read your tide tables

Charts 3463 Strait of Georgia, Southern Portion, 1:80,000
3490 Fraser River, Sand Heads to Douglas Island, 1:20,000
3492 Roberts Bank, 1:20,000

Launching and take-out sites

This trip is designed to begin at the Deas Slough in Deas Island Regional Park, adjacent to the Delta Deas Island Rowing Club. There is a low dock there that provides easy launching, and a small section of shore is also accessible immediately to the left of the dock for those more comfortable launching from a beach. Launching is also possible at the government dock at the foot of Elliot Street on Ladner Reach, in downtown Ladner. You can also do the trip in reverse from the suggested take-out at Wellington Point Park, where there is a cement boat ramp and dock.

Getting there

This trip can be done as a return trip or with two vehicles, making it an easy two-hour float downstream on an outgoing tide.

To get to Deas Island Regional Park take the River Road east exit at the Highway 99/Highway 17 junction, southeast of the George Massey Tunnel. Follow signs to Deas Island Regional Park. The distance from the

Guide continues on p. 121

Ladner's Landing as seen from a departing ferry, ca. 1890. Photo courtesy Delta Museum and Archives.

AN EVOLVING HISTORY OF DELTA, DEAS ISLAND AND LADNER

THE EARLY HISTORY OF DELTA revolves around the abundance of salmon, shellfish, wildlife and berries that could be easily gathered or caught. Despite now being one of the most fertile areas in British Columbia, before diking the interior of the delta area was swampy, water-logged and prone to flooding. Both the Tsawwassen First Nations and the settlers who arrived in 1859 camped or built homes along the river's edge or along the two large sloughs (Crescent and Chilukthan)

***History* continues on p. 122**

junction to the park turn-off is about 2 km. The rowing club boathouse is the first building on the south side of the road as you enter the park.

To get to the Elliot Street dock and Wellington Point Park from the George Massey Tunnel, take the River Road south exit immediately after you come out of the tunnel. Follow River Road for about 2 km to where it runs directly into Elliot Street. Turn right and you are there.

To get to Wellington Point Park, turn left at Elliot Street and then right at the 47A Avenue/Ladner Trunk Road junction about 250 m south. Follow 47A Avenue west. After about 800 m it will turn into River Road West. Continue a further 2.5 km. Wellington Point Park will be on your right.

If you are coming from the south or east, turn onto Ladner Trunk Road from Highway 17, 1.7 km south of the Highway 99/Highway 17 junction. Follow the Ladner Trunk Road west for about 2 km to its junction with Elliot Street and 47A Avenue. Go straight across, and after about 800 m, 47A Avenue will turn into River Road West. Continue west a further 2.5 km. Wellington Point Park will be on your right.

Parking

Parking is free in the Deas Island Regional Park parking lot, by the rowing club. There is free on-street parking in the vicinity of the Elliot Street dock. There is also plenty of free parking at Wellington Point Park.

Washrooms

The Deas Island Regional Park has washrooms. There are none at Wel-

lington Park (the turnaround point), however, so you are left with going behind the bushes on various sandy islands along the way. At low tide the silt soil is very sticky on these islands.

Paddling considerations

Tides and river currents are the primary concern here. Check your tide table or consult the local kayak shop on the best time to paddle before you set out. While the Ladner area is generally ideal for kayaking, with sheltered waters and few waves, storms can occasionally blow in over the low-lying islands from the Strait of Georgia. Fishing boats, pleasure boats, rowing sculls, water skiers, jet skis and very shallow areas between the sandy, uninhabited islands during low tide should also be kept in mind.

There are guidelines in place for the use of Deas Slough to avoid conflicts between motorized and non-motorized watercraft. For more information, contact the Fraser River Port Authority at 604-524-6655.

The route

When you are getting ready to launch your kayak, you can look to the north and see the south arm of the Fraser River. There is a reason why you are not launching on this side of the island. The fast current and the numerous ocean freighters making their way up the South Fraser make this a route full of challenges, often very large, moving, four-storey-high challenges! The Fraser River Port Authority does not want kayakers on the south arm of the Fraser at all. In fact it does not

Guide continues on p. 123

Deas Island Slough to Wellington Point Park – 121

Deas Island cannery on northwest point of the island, ca. 1920s. Photo courtesy Delta Museum and Archives.

rather than live on the central part of the delta or farm the soggy soil.

Early settlers began to pre-empt land, taking advantage of a practice adopted by the government to cope with the land needs of the influx of people during the gold rush. Settlers were allowed to live on and clear unsurveyed land without any payment until the surveying was done. A number of homesteads were located between Brownsville (opposite New Westminster) and the mouth of the Fraser between 1860 and 1868, but nearly all of them were abandoned. It wasn't until after the Ladner brothers, William and Thomas, laid claim to large tracts of land in 1868 that the development of the Delta area escalated. The building of roads also helped decrease dependence on the waterways for the shipment of goods and increase communication and movement of people between settlements. By 1880 all the land in the Delta peninsula had been pre-empted except for the bog area. For each farmer the initial task was to build dikes, first around their homes and then in the area where they intended to farm. It was not until the spring of 1894,

History **continues on p. 124**

even like having large tour boats using the river from New Westminster to the mouth of the river at Steveston.

Beside the launch area is the Delta Deas Rowing Club, which started in 1986 as a 1500-m practice setting for high-school rowers. The club has grown to over 100 members of every age and skill level and trains both competitive and recreational rowers.

On Deas Island you can see several heritage buildings that have been moved there from other areas of Delta. The Inverholme Schoolhouse, built in 1909, was moved to the Island from Boundary Bay in 1981. Also in 1981, Burrvilla, a Queen Anne style house, was moved from the South River Road. The park maintenance building is housed in the Delta Agricultural Hall, which first opened in Ladner in 1899.

It was on the tip of the north side of Deas Island that John Sullivan Deas built dikes and then in 1873 started B.C.'s second salmon cannery. John Sullivan Deas was the first settler on the Island. He was a "free black" who had immigrated with a number of blacks who arrived in the Victoria area from the U.S. after that country's Civil War. Deas ran the cannery successfully for five years, often producing the most cases of salmon of any of the canneries on the Fraser. When he failed to get exclusive fishing rights in the area of the cannery, he sold his interests and returned to the U.S. The island became home first to the people working in the canneries and then to many Greek families who fished individually with gillnetters. The last inhabitants on the island lived there until the early 1950s.

Paddle down the slough, and at low tide on the south shore just before the RiverHouse condominium development, marina and restaurant, you can see the hull of an old boat.

Pass under the Highway 99 ramp to the George Massey Tunnel, often known as the Deas Island Tunnel. George Massey was a Social Credit MLA who spent years campaigning for the tunnel's construction. The six precast units that make up the tunnel were floated into position and sunk into place in the river bed. At that time little concern was given to seismic specifications, but you will be glad to know, if you drive Highway 99 very often, that a structural upgrading to meet seismic standards will be completed in the spring of 2006.

From 1913 until the opening of the Massey tunnel in 1958, there was a ferry crossing the river that could transport 70 cars an hour. Starting at the end of Ferry Road slightly west of Captain's Cove Marina, it went over to Woodward's Landing further west in Richmond. This took an hour off the trip to Vancouver compared to the other route from Ladner via Steveston.

On the south is Captain's Cove Marina and on the north is a small island with deciduous trees. It is only at low tide that you can see that this entire "island" is growing on an old wooden barge.

As you leave the slough area, look north and you will often see large BC Ferries vessels in the dock for repairs. The government company that began in 1960 with two ships and two terminals, at Horseshoe Bay and

Guide continues on p. 125

when dikes broke and the whole area got flooded, that the municipality finally assumed responsibility for diking.

The early history of this area also is the history of salmon canning. Large salmon runs occurred in the areas of Canoe Pass, the South Fraser mouth and off Point Roberts' southeastern tip. Preserving fish in the 1860s consisted of salting and curing it. The development of canning precipitated the construction of numerous canneries from Wellington Point at the eastern end of Canoe Pass all the way to New Westminster. Once canning was introduced, an additional workforce was needed to meet the world-wide demand, and First Nations people and Chinese were employed. The Chinese workers were especially valued, since they were very dexterous in creating the can seam and then soldering the seams to seal the cans. A Chinese community developed in Ladner and around the other canneries as more people immigrated and found work there. It was a competitive business dependent upon the size of the salmon run, but in those days there were plenty of fish and plenty of investors.

Although in the early 1900s whole sockeye salmon were selling for 10 cents apiece, spring salmon for 3 cents and pinks two for a nickel, canning added value and the canned product could be exported all over the world. Ladner became the pivotal canning centre along the Fraser River and by 1899, when the industry peaked, there were 16 canneries located between Annieville, close to New Westminster, and Canoe Pass, west of Ladner.

The combined resources of salmon and agriculture ensured population growth of the area in the early years and still contribute to Delta's economy today.

❧

Old Peter Grimes made fishing his employ;
His wife he cabined with him and his boy,
And seemed that life laborious to enjoy.

from Peter Grimes,
by George Crabbe (1754–1832)

Swartz Bay, is now a privately owned company with 35 vessels and up to 47 ports of call.

Do not go out into the main channel; stay to your left past Kirkland, Williamson and Gunn Islands as you paddle along the marsh on your south. The islands shift in shape as the soil is deposited or taken away each day. Several of the islands have a house or two on them and the docks are private, so do not land.

The southern shore has several wildlife viewing stations. This area is part of the Ladner Marsh and the South Arm Marshes Wildlife Management Area, which includes all of the land between Deas Island and Westham Island. Paddling among these islands, you are more likely to see a variety of birds in the quieter waters. Remember your way back from between the islands, and be aware that if you get out to stretch on one that is not inhabited, the soil along the shoreline is often like glue.

By staying to the left in the main channel, you are in Ladner Reach. You can turn in to the waterway that parallels the older part of the village and paddle to the end of the inlet, where you will soon reach the waterfront of Ladner Village. In the late 1800s this area could be accessed by a deep channel on this south side of the Fraser River, which has long since silted up. This silt helped create the land to the north of the channel on which Ladner Harbour Park now sits and makes this area an inlet rather than an open channel. William Ladner donated land at the mouth of the Chilukthan Slough to build a government dock. It was soon called

Ladner's Landing and became the only stop made by steamers between Victoria and New Westminster.

The village is named after the Ladner brothers, William and Thomas, who, after adventures in the gold fields and building a business in New Westminster, were in 1868 among the first settlers to begin farming at the mouth of the delta. They pre-empted land on either side of the Chilukthan slough and then expanded their holdings from there. The Ladner family were leaders in agricultural, community and political affairs. William Ladner developed part of his homestead as a community post office and would ferry mail to and from passing steamers. In addition to being postmaster, William was also justice of the peace, the municipality's first reeve and a member in the first Legislative Assembly. Thomas farmed, built the Delta Cannery at the mouth of the slough, and later became manager of the Wellington Cannery and part owner of five canneries. With the energy that seemed to run in his family, Thomas, in his late 40s, married a girl of 16.

The Ladner brothers were joined by many other pioneers who settled along the two major sloughs and the Fraser River, since these water routes offered the only reliable means of transportation of goods or people. After the initial land was cleared for family needs, many of the settlers chose to raise livestock. There was a steady market in Victoria and New Westminster for any surplus produce and meat.

There are numerous fishing boats moored in this channel, just as there

A kayaker's quick guide to fish boats

Seiners, trawlers, gillnetters, longliners—what *is* the difference?

Trolling catches the fish on hooks towed behind the boat, with modern boats having up to 120 lures dangling at one time. These boats are easily recognized by their long, thin outrigger poles. When a troller is at the dock, these poles would be standing straight up.

Not to be confused with trollers, trawlers use a cone-shaped net dragged beneath the surface mid-water and along the bottom to catch pollock, groundfish and shrimp. This is perhaps the most controversial method of fishing, since it results in much bycatch in addition to the desired species. There is also concern about the effect on the ocean floor from dragging the trawl nets along. You can recognize a trawler by the large net reel on its stern.

Longlining uses long lines with baited hooks that sit on the ocean floor and catch bottom-feeders such as halibut. The longline is pulled back onto a revolving drum or piled on the deck by a powered winch.

Gillnetting uses a horizontal net held at the top by floats and set perpendicular to the direction the fish are swimming. These boats have a large hydraulic drum with the net stored on it at the back of the boat. When the net is pulled in, the fish are picked out of it.

Seiners encircle the fish with a net which is then gathered and pulled together at the bottom edge. These boats also have a drum or hydraulically powered block to pull in the net.

It was not until the 1950s that nets were made of synthetic materials. Previously they were of linen, which needed drying sheds and strong fishermen to drag them in by hand.

Spot the Hobbit house among the floating homes at Port Guichon.

Fishboats riding at anchor on the Ladner waterfront

were when Ladner's Landing served a pivotal maritime and economic role in the delta region.

When you return from the trip past the Ladner waterfront, continue on the left side of the channel. You will pass by numerous floating homes situated in front of the dikes. This too has historical precedent. Many of the salmon fishermen lived in float homes that could be moved along the river, and the early settlers at Port Guichon are reported to have lived in scow houses while fishing from skiffs. The floating homes are grouped in the communities of River Run, Port Guichon and Canoe Pass (which is after the Westham Island Bridge), and the variety of house styles is limited only by the imagination of their owners. See if you can spot the one that may have a Hobbit living in it, close to the dike in the Port Guichon area.

Port Guichon is just before the large Lions Gate fish processing plant. In 1883 Laurent Guichon, an entrepreneur from the Savoy region of France, had already successfully started a hotel in New Westminster when he moved to this area. He established a hotel, store and wharf at Port Guichon and operated a large farm. He was joined by other immigrants, primarily from Croatia, who brought such skills as shipbuilding to the community. A sawmill on the banks of the dikes also added employment opportunities.

The wharf at both Ladner's Landing and Port Guichon served as a dock for boats loading cases of salmon from the nearby canneries. The Port Guichon dock was also used for ferries between Steveston on the north shore of the south arm of the Fraser River. As well, a rail ferry sailed from here to Sidney on Vancouver Island.

SS Victorian *and the square-rigger* Forteviot *docked at Port Guichon with a train waiting on the wharf, ca. 1903. Photo courtesy Delta Museum and Archives.*

The whole train would be put aboard the ferry and taken across.

When rail lines opened to Port Guichon from Cloverdale in the Fraser Valley in 1903 and from Chilliwack in 1909, it increased communication and commerce somewhat between the two areas, but the trip was long and the schedule limited. It was not until roads were built offering more reliable access that Delta became a more popular community. Even today the western part of Delta maintains its rural atmosphere and lifestyle.

After passing by Port Guichon, at the eastern end of Canoe Pass, you will see a large jetty, which is part of the Wellington Point Park. There is a boat launch there and picnic tables, so this may be a good spot to stretch and have a snack. The large Wellington

Cannery was built here in 1880. It had 245 employees and could produce 12,000 cases of salmon a year.

Down Canoe Pass south of Wellington Point Park a bridge crosses over to Westham Island. The Island is part of Delta Municipality and had a similar economic development. Salmon canneries and farms existed in the diked areas; and fish camps, whose occupants supplied the canneries, developed in the areas that remained subject to flooding. The George C. Reifel Migratory Bird Sanctuary, at the northeast end of the Island, was created in 1960 when Reifel's son first leased the land his father had owned on the tip of Westham Island to the British Columbia Waterfowl Society. Later in 1972 he combined donations with sale of land to include the family homestead, waterways and farm fields to conserve the land as a bird sanctuary. The farm area is now called the Alaksen National Wildlife Area.

The Reifel family are generally remembered for this significant donation, but they also contributed to local history in another way. George Reifel raised sugar beets, and during the Second World War he produced over one-third of all Canadian sugar beet seed. As well, the next time you lift a lager, toast the Reifels: they founded the Vancouver Breweries, which was later named the O'Keefe Brewery.

A note on wildlife viewing on this trip: If you can ignore the noisy jetskiers among the islands, there are many other, more interesting things to watch. Although seals are the most frequent animal you will see on this marine trail, do not be surprised if you see a much larger head. Sea Lions are occasionally sighted in the Canoe Pass region and often in front of the fish processing plant close to Wellington Park Wharf. Since over 240 species of birds have been identified at the Reifel Migratory Sanctuary, bird watching could also be a full day's activity.

You may want to paddle out to the end of Canoe Pass before turning around. This passageway was named in 1858 by the gold miners who were heading to the riches of the Cariboo goldfields. It looks onto the Strait of Georgia, named by Captain Vancouver for his king, the "mad" King George III.

Time to return and explore the Delta landscape and historic buildings from the land.

Wellington Cannery at Canoe Pass, ca. 1890. To the left of the nets drying on racks in the foreground are men mending nets. On the right are workers' huts.

Victoria's Inner Harbour, looking north from the Legislature, ca. 1900. Photo courtesy Vancouver Public Library.

A PROPER HISTORY
OF EARLY VICTORIA

FORT VICTORIA WAS ESTABLISHED IN 1843 by the Chief Factor of the Hudson's Bay Company (HBC), James Douglas, on Lekwungen (Songhees) territory called Camosun or Camosack. The name was given to the entire area although it referred to the reversing falls at the narrowing of The Gorge waterway and meant "rushing water." The trading post was first called Fort Camosun, but by mid-1843 it was renamed Fort Victoria to honour the Queen. The immediate area around the Fort was called Ku-sing-ay-las (place of strong fibre) by the Songhees, for the strong willow tree fibre that had, among other benefits, the strength to be used as rope ties on stones to create sinkers for deep-sea fishing. The

History continues on p. 132

10 Victoria Inner and Middle Harbour

Difficulty Beginner conditions – low risk

Distances 3 nmi from Songhees Point via James Bay to Shoal Point and back
2 nmi from Songhees Point to West Bay and back

Duration 2–3 hours round trip

Charts 3415 Victoria Harbour, 1:6,000
3440 Race Rocks to D'Arcy Island, 1:40,000
Small-Craft Nautical Map Set A

Launching and take-out sites

While the Victoria harbour is an important historical and present-day destination and is filled with boats of all sizes, harbour ferries and sea planes, little thought has gone into providing easy access to the water for paddlers. The beach south of the Delta Ocean Pointe Resort on Songhees Point is your best choice for direct access to the harbour. It is a short carry from the road to a sandy beach tucked beside the rocks of the point. The other access points are from the docks of many nearby kayak rental businesses located on the Inner, Middle and Upper harbours. Phone ahead, as some will charge launching fees for non-renters. Contact information is listed in the resource section of this book. The James Bay Anglers Club boat launch in the Outer Harbour between Shoal and Ogden Points is another option to explore.

Getting there

Songhees Point—From downtown Victoria take the Johnson Street Bridge (blue bridge), and after passing under the railway bridge on the Esquimalt side, turn left onto Tyee Road, which will then turn into Songhees Road. The launch point will be visible on your left below the highly visible totem pole.

Parking

Free parking is available on the streets nearby the Delta Ocean Pointe Resort. Note that parking is free all day Sunday and for 2 ½ to 3 ½ hours Monday through Saturday. If you are launching from a rental location, inquire with the outfitter for your best option, but expect to have to pay at most locations.

Washrooms

Delta Ocean Pointe Resort is very kind in allowing use of their lower-level washrooms, through the ground level café. Try not to track sand and water into their facility. Most of the rental locations have washroom facilities.

Paddling considerations

The Victoria harbour is a very busy place, with harbour ferries, international passenger and car ferries,

Guide continues on p. 133

Songhees lived in three areas around the fort: just east of Laurel Point, across the Harbour in the area of the Johnson Street Bridge and on the eastern shore beside the fort.

Fort Victoria was operated for the next 20 years as an HBC monopoly under the leadership of James Douglas. The Songhees people played a pivotal role in the early years. Not only did they cut down the trees to build the fort, but it was their skill at trapping and hunting that provided the otter and beaver pelts and whale oil for trading export.

James Douglas was often regarded as an inflexible tyrant during his days with the HBC and as governor of the new colonies of Vancouver Island in 1849 and British Columbia in 1858. However, he was insistent that the native people be treated as free British subjects who had legal rights. He negotiated 14 treaties with Indian bands on southern Vancouver Island, including the Esquimalt land title. By 1910 the last remaining Songhees tribe members had each been paid $10,000 and moved to the new reserve in Esquimalt, much to the relief of the townspeople, who saw the native settlements as examples of vice and depravity. There was, of course, another agenda. Once the native settlements were removed, the surrounding areas with their ready access to the harbour were turned into industrial developments.

The 1858 gold rush into the Fraser Valley and the 1897–98 one to the Klondike saw dramatic development in Victoria. Victoria was usually the first port of entry for the gold miners and the place where they bought their initial provisions. During the gold rush days, the citizens of Victoria were appalled by the lives and behaviours of the gold miners who invaded their city. However, despite the citizens' protestations of

History **continues on p. 134**

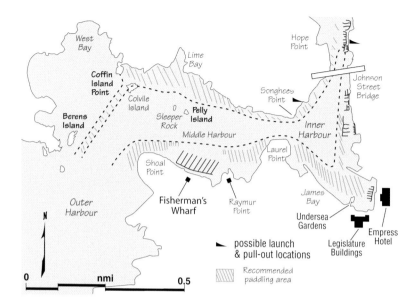

West
Bay

Hope
Point

Lime
Bay

**Coffin
Island
Point**

Johnson
Street
Bridge

Colvile
Island

Songhees
Point

**Berens
Island**

Sleeper
Rock

**Pelly
Island**

Inner
Harbour

Middle Harbour

Laurel
Point

Shoal
Point

Outer
Harbour

Fisherman's
Wharf

Raymur
Point

James
Bay

Undersea
Gardens

N

Legislature
Buildings

Empress
Hotel

➤ possible launch
& pull-out locations

Recommended
paddling area

0   nmi   0.5

pleasure craft, rowers, canoeists, kayakers, float planes taxiing and taking off, tugs and ships coming to the shipyards for repairs. To keep all this traffic in line, Transport Canada and the Port of Victoria have put in place a "traffic scheme." Generally it means that kayakers must remain as close to shore as possible so that they do not interfere with commercial vessels.

Specific regulations state that non-motorized vessels must remain north of the white and orange buoy located just south of the Songhees Point shoreline. While in the Middle Harbour, vessels must remain north of Pelly Island and close to the north shore west of Colvile Island. On the south side of the Middle Harbour, vessels must stay as close to the south shore as possible.

Crossing the Middle Harbour is not permitted at any time, so to get from Songhees Point to Laurel Point you must paddle around the perimeter of the Inner Harbour and James Bay, preferably crossing the harbour north of the Johnson Street Bridge. It is also recommended that when transiting from the Upper to Inner Harbour (i.e., under the Johnson Street bridge), kayakers stay to the west of the wooden fender piles under the bridge. A handout is available from most kayak rental shops detailing the restrictions, or you can call the Harbour Master directly at 250-363-3578. You can also view and download the handout on the Transport Canada web site, www.tc.gc.ca/pacific/marine/victoriaharbourtrafficscheme.htm.

Guide continues on p. 135

social and racial superiority, the city was very much a mixed population, with James Douglas himself being married to a woman of First Nations (Cree) and European origin. In addition to the First Nations, Victoria's Chinese population made up the second largest Chinatown in North America (after San Francisco). The arrival of over 250 "free blacks" who emigrated from the u.s. after that country's Civil War added to the ethnic mix. All of these immigrants contributed to the growth of the city, and several rose to prominence in city politics.

Stores, warehouses, hotels and bars were established to serve the needs of the gold miners as well as the loggers and cannery workers. Businesses flourished within the developing city, including breweries, flour mills, boot and shoe, harness and door and stair manufacturers, as well as clothiers, soap works and shipyards. Victoria also became the main port for export of the thousands of cases of canned salmon that were produced in the canneries of the Fraser River.

As Vancouver rose in prominence, and with the choice of Vancouver as the terminus of the Trans-Canada railway, Victoria faded in economic importance. Fortunately, because Victoria was maintained as the provincial capital and thus the centre of British Columbia's politics, as well as having developed a strong tourist base, it continues to gain recognition by visitors and locals alike.

જ્જ

The route

From Songhees Point, cross directly over toward the green grass park situated on the east side of the harbour. This park is known as Reeson Regional Park, and in the summer the smell of another kind of grass may reach you on the water. On the building along the park's south side you can see fading pictures of whales, painted in 1987 by Robert Wyland and dedicated to Robin Morton, a researcher into whale behaviour and communication, who died in 1986. Wyland first started painting whales on the walls of public buildings in 1981 when he took six months to paint life-size whales on a wall in Laguna Beach, California. He completes his work for free, with the aid of volunteers and sponsors, and independently chooses the public spaces where he will paint. By 2008 he intends to have 100 "whaling walls" completed and he now finishes some walls within a week. This is whaling wall #13, so Victoria, along with White Rock (wall #4) and Vancouver (#8), were early in the series of 91 international cities that have Wyland whales on their city buildings. The painter's work is supported by the Wyland Foundation, which helps to spread the message Wyland intends by painting the pictures. He initially started painting the whales and dolphins to show their delicate beauty and to contribute to efforts to save them, but now he says his primary focus has broadened to increasing awareness of the need to save the oceans to be able to save ourselves.

Bastion Square is an open space in the buildings facing the harbour. On the left you will see tall trees, on the right a red brick building and beside it one with ornate windows and white and black paint. These heritage buildings were completely derelict in 1973, when luckily the city decided to rehabilitate them. Bastion Square marks the location of where Fort Victoria stood. A double row of 2,535 bricks, set in the sidewalk and engraved with the names of citizens who lived in Victoria before 1914, outlines where the stockade surrounding the 91×152-metre quadrangle existed. The fort was destroyed in 1860–61 to make room for new businesses. Bastion Square also marks the location where the 27 hangings ordered by Judge Matthew Baillie Begbie occurred. Consequently Bastion Square has its fair share of ghosts. John Adams, ghost-master of Victoria, describes a wealth of ghosts in the buildings, hotels and homes of Victoria during his daily summer tours.

During the time the fort was standing, there were two octagonal bastions projecting from the north (rear) and south (front) corners of its fortifications, which were made up of cedar posts approximately 4.5 m high. The Songhees were "paid" in blankets and goods to cut down and provide the posts from Mount Douglas. The bastions were built to view an approaching enemy and to gain height for shooting the cannons that were inside. During the time the fort was standing, there were several attacks by First Nations tribes but none by foreign armies or navies, so the soldiers who lived in the Bachelor's Hall of the fort were left with spare time to entertain themselves. This included attending balls on visiting ships in the harbour and following the rigid schedule and activities set out by Governor James Douglas, the original founder of the fort in 1843 and "ruler" until his retirement in 1864.

A red, bricked-in archway, now well back from the shoreline where it originally stood, indicates the location of the door to the Hudson's Bay Company warehouse. Built in 1854, this was the first commercial building constructed in Victoria. It provided imported goods and supplies to settlers and citizens for over 70 years.

A pink-coloured brick building is on the shore close to the water. This was the original Customs House (1002 Wharf Street), built by the federal government in 1875, four years after British Columbia entered Confederation. (Having had to pay off the provincial debt to convince British Columbia to join Confederation, the federal government used customs duties as one way to get the money back.) The customs house has a distinctive French "mansard" architectural style which was popular in Eastern Canada and the U.S. in the late 1800s after Napoleon III rebuilt Paris using it. The style originated with architect François Mansart (1598–1666) during the French Renaissance and is seen in parts of the Louvre. Mansard roofs have a steep-sloped lower section with dormers and a shallower-sloped upper section, which gives commercial buildings the advantage of extra space above. The present-day

Seaplane taxiing past the original, mansard-roofed Customs House in Victoria's Inner Harbour

Fort Victoria and the bottom of Fort Street, ca. 1840s. Photo courtesy British Columbia Archives.

customs building is on the south side of the harbour where the international passenger and car ferries arrive.

Along the stone wall below the fort area, you can still see a large iron ring where ships would tie up while their cargo was declared at the nearby customs house and unloaded into the fort or the Hudson's Bay Company store. As late as 1911, sealing and whaling ships used the harbour for moorage and unloading cargo.

You will pass by several seaplane bases (Hyak, Kenmore, Westcoast Air and Harbour Air). Be alert to when planes are being untied to take off, and wait until they leave before going in front of their dock space. Their pilots have the novelty of landing on the runways of the only sea-based international airport in Canada. The planes have two runways, Alpha and Bravo, through the centre of the Outer and Middle Harbours, and they taxi into and out of the Inner Harbour. There are over 26,000 landings and takeoffs a year, often more than 120 a day. Seaplanes have landed in the harbour since the 1930s and there has never been a fatality. In early harbour days, clipper ships, sternwheelers and other boats would have moored in the same place as the seaplanes.

As you paddle around the harbour, you will also see numerous Harbour Ferries scooting about. (They are allowed to cross the seaplane runway at one point only; but remember, you are not!) Their guides give informative tours about the history and places in the harbour and up The Gorge, but you will not need that now!

Every Sunday morning at 9:45 from mid-June until mid-September

Two of the many Harbour Ferries that scoot about Victoria Harbour . . .
and waltz on summer Sunday mornings before the Empress Hotel

the ferries waltz to the Blue Danube in front of the Empress Hotel. These ferries were designed by the same boat builder who made the ferries that are used in Vancouver's False Creek.

As you round the corner you will see the part of Government Street that once formed the causeway to James Bay. At water level below Government Street is a pedestrian walkway in front of the Empress. Many of the stones in the wall at the water edge of the lower causeway were once ballast stones from the ships that sailed to Victoria from Europe.

There is often at least one tall ship moored along the north side of the harbour. The *Pacific Swift* was built on the Expo fairgrounds during Expo 86 and has since sailed more than 100,000 nmi. Both it and the *Pacific Grace* serve as training ships for SALTS (the Sail and Life Training Society). The society is a non-profit Christian organization that provides coastal and offshore sailing training and education programs for adolescents. Look for carvings along the sides of the *Pacific Grace* and the carved figurehead on the bow of the *Pacific Swift*. Occasionally the *Robertson II* is also moored at this dock. It operated as a fishing boat off the coast of Newfoundland and later became a SALTS ship. It has now been purchased by private enterprise.

At the northern corner of the harbour pedestrian walkway is a building that presently houses the Tourism Victoria Information Centre. It was built in 1931 as the Imperial Oil Tower and housed a three-level garage and ferry terminal. The beacon on the top could be seen for up to 100 km and was used to shine flood lights on the Imperial Oil sign close by and to guide seaplanes landing at night in the Inner Harbour. Needless to say, during the Second World War the lights were not allowed to be on.

Present day Government Street (above the north/south pedestrian walkway) was originally just a bridge to get over the two hectares of mudflats at the end of James Bay and to the community around the Parliament Buildings.

A causeway was built and the mud flats were filled in during 1859 and then thousands of 90-foot logs were sunk into the mud to act as pillars on which to support the Empress Hotel. Consequently, from time to time these supports have to be reinforced to prevent the Empress from tilting over. After all, the Empress is famous for her afternoon teas rather than tippling in alcoholic beverages. More than 800 people a day come to enjoy the experience of an authentic English tea in the Tea Lobby.

A young English architect, Francis Rattenbury (who also designed the British Columbia legislature buildings and the building that now houses the Wax Museum), used an adapted version of the popular chateau style favoured by the Canadian Pacific Railway owners, when he designed the Empress. The hotel was opened in 1908 with additions in 1910, 1913 and 1929. A $45 million dollar face-lift, that restored the "heart and soul of the city" to its former elegance, was completed in 1989. Stories of ghosts have been told about the Empress: a little girl who floats across a bedroom, and a 20th-century maid who still feels compelled to help with cleaning on the sixth floor.

In the summer, the harbour walkway is filled with colour. Buskers, boats, ferries, and best of all, some of the 1,200 beautiful hanging flower baskets that can be seen here and throughout the city. The baskets, containing a selection of about 25 varieties of plants, were first introduced in 1937 to celebrate the 75th anniversary of Victoria becoming a city.

At the south end of the harbour are the provincial legislature buildings. The buildings were constructed between 1893 and 1896, at a cost of $923,000, which was two-thirds of the annual revenue of the province at that time! Preceding the present buildings, the original legislative buildings were five buildings built in 1859 and called the "birdcages" because of their unusual architectural style. They were described by the local newspaper, *The Gazette*, as having elements of Chinese pagoda, Swiss cottage and Italian villa birdcages all painted in rather startling contrast of deep red with white trim paint. These buildings were originally planned to be in the main downtown area, but by the time they were built in the 1860s, the land was too expensive due to inflation from the gold rush boom, and so the less expensive area in James Bay was used.

The legislature buildings were first illuminated at night in 1897 for

Queen Victoria's Diamond Jubilee to distract from the fact that they were not completed structurally in time for the event, and since 1956 have been outlined nightly by over 3,330 light bulbs. On a sunny day the 24-carat gilded statue of Captain Vancouver shines beacon-like and looks down from the centre cupola. Other statues lingering around the lawn are of Queen Victoria, Captain Cook and James Douglas, who was governor of the colony of Vancouver Island from 1851 and of British Columbia to 1864 after amalgamation with the mainland. Under the lawn are tunnels, once used by New Democratic members to hide and then storm the legislative assembly after tricking the Social Credit party into calling a vote with too few of their members present (it didn't work). On either side of the main entrance are Captain George Vancouver (left side) and Judge Matthew Baillie Begbie (right side), who, as he meted out justice throughout British Columbia, was often called the "hanging judge." This name was enhanced by his statements such as "Aye, we'll give ye a fair trial and then we'll hang ye."

To the far right of the legislature lawns is a Knowledge totem pole carved by Cicero August and his sons, of the Cowichan tribes. This was to celebrate the closing of the XIVth Commonwealth Games in Auckland, New Zealand, and the beginning of Victoria's hosting of the games in August 1994. The figures depicted on the pole are a loon, a fisherman, a bone game player and a frog, who represent lessons of the past and hope for the future.

At 3 pm on Sundays from April to December, and at 7 pm on Fridays from July to August, you may hear the Netherlands Centennial Carillon that stands beside the museum. The bells were a gift in 1967 from British Columbians of Dutch origin to celebrate Canada's centennial year. Now with 62 bells, (originally 49), this carillon is right up there with the world's largest. Music can be played in any key, since the bells of a carillon are arranged in chromatic sequence, including sharps and flats. The bells are tuned to produce concordant harmony when many bells are sounded together. The carillon bells are fixed to a metal frame and clappers strike the inside of the bell to create the music. The clappers are attached to wires and a tracker system that leads to a keyboard. As well, the larger bells are attached to foot pedals. The carillon keyboard is struck with a half-closed hand, with musical expression produced by variation in touch.

To the east of the legislature buildings is the Royal British Columbia Museum. In 1887 the precursor of this building was opened in the "Birdcages" as the British Columbia Museum of Natural History and Anthropology. The early curator, John Fannin, had such a fondness for stuffed animals that most of the early exhibits consisted of British Columbia zoological specimens. Fannin had little interest in gathering cultural items for the museum, so while he used to go on specific hunting trips to augment his animal and fossil collections, hundreds of collectors from Europe and the United States descended on British Columbia to get samples of totem poles, native relics and even bones of First Nations peoples. A director of the museum in the early 1900s , Frank Kermode, spent a great deal of time trying to get samples and information on the white bear found only on Princess Royal Island and in the Terrace area. The Kermode bear, or Great Spirit bear, was named after him. The present museum, opened in 1968, now houses the original botanical and fossil artifacts and historical items, as well as three-dimensional historical scenes of local and provincial interest, such as a Kwakiutl longhouse. Visiting displays are launched each year just in time for tourist season. From the water you will be able to see large banners on the side of the museum announcing them.

Beside the museum is Helmcken House, built in 1852 as the home for Dr. John Sebastian Helmcken, who was the first physician for the Hudson's Bay Company. Governor Douglas and Dr. Helmcken had two of the first houses to be built outside the fort. Douglas gave the land to Helmcken, who became his son-in-law. Some of the original log structure can be seen inside and it contains some furnishings and objects such as the original medicine chest owned by Helmcken. The house has been open to the public since 1941, when the provincial government began restorations.

The Pacific Undersea Gardens appear to float in the harbour just before the Royal London Wax Museum. When visitors are viewing some of the 5,000 animals in the displays at the lowest level, they are 5 m beneath the ocean. There are viewing windows that allow visitors to look into the ocean waters beneath your kayak and view marine life. Be careful around here… Someone is watching your bottom!

The Royal London Wax Museum is in the cement building with 23 tall Ionic columns and bas-relief designs of the Greek sea god Poseidon and dolphins. It was a last architectural hurrah for Francis Rattenbury, who in 1924 designed it as a departure and arrivals building for the Canadian Pacific Railway coastal passenger steamships and ocean liners christened with a "Princess" in their name. After years of varied use and disuse, the lower floor was reborn as the Wax Museum. One of its wax people sitting in the lobby is lifelike enough to encourage you to talk to him.

Recently, world-renowned Vancouver architect Arthur Erickson suggested that to enhance the harbour, the building should be returned to its former use as a terminal for passengers arriving on the numerous international ferries that dock in Victoria.

These huge ferries are your next navigational challenge. The largest of them is MV *Coho*, which shuttles passenger cars between Victoria and Port Angeles, Washington. It is operated by the U.S. Blackball Ferry Company and locals call it the "Blackball Ferry." This is a curious name that warrants investigation. Is there gambling on the ship? Billiards, maybe? The history of the Blackball Line dates back to 1807, when the company took over a variety of trans-Atlantic clipper ship lines. The Blackball Line established itself as not only one of the biggest clipper ship lines but also the fastest between Boston and London and between Liverpool and New York. In 1817 the company established a regular schedule ensuring arrival of goods within a specific time. The "black ball" name comes from dial clocks first introduced in the 1720s which had a simple, round, black face (a black ball) with brass numerals. Both stage coaches and shipping lines used these clocks to advertise their businesses and imply reliability.

Some other ferries you may see include the *Victoria Clipper*, a high speed catamaran that takes foot passengers to Seattle and the San Juan Islands, and the *Victoria Star*, which shuttles foot passengers between Bellingham, Washington, and Victoria. The *Victoria Express*, also a foot passenger ferry, links Victoria, Friday Harbour and Port Angeles, Washington.

Once you pass the ferries you will see Laurel Point, which was an important burial and living area for the Songhees. Laurel is another name for the arbutus trees that grew in that area. In the mid-1800s burial houses and grave figures were located here. There were four carved and painted human figures standing on the point, representing the dead chiefs buried there. Consequently, the settlers called it Deadman's Point. In the late 1870s William Pendray established his British Columbia Soapworks on the Point, producing up to 9,000 pounds of White Swan soap every day. He later established the Bapco Paint Company, which remained on the point until 1965. These factories were only two

Between constant seaplane traffic and ferries large and small, Victoria's harbour is a very busy place.

among many shipyards, sawmills and machine shops that lined the entrance to the Inner Harbour in the 1880s. Pendray's ornate white house (the Queen Anne style Gatsby House and Restaurant in front of the Ramada Huntington Hotel and Suites) remains in its original location. It is said that Pendray, who died when a pipe in his factory fell 40 feet and hit his head, haunts the former master bedroom. As well, the presence of one of the household maids is felt (or seen) on the entrance stairway. The factories the house once overlooked have been replaced by the Laurel Point Inn. Its ship-like design faces the harbour and Centennial Park/Laurel Point Park. A walkway runs around the point.

You will pass by the Coast Harbourside Hotel marina floats and Raymur Point on your way to Fisherman's Wharf. It is a Victoria Harbour Authority dock and floating home area. Piers 1, 2 and 3 have permanent houseboats. If you paddle in to the shore area of the docks, you may be able to have what some consider the best fish and chips in Victoria. Certainly the friendly seals that occasionally hang around here looking for a free meal seem to enjoy the leftovers.

In the area of Fisherman's Wharf and Shoal Point is the new Shoal Point Development where the Chevron bulk oil plant was formerly situated. Now with 151 condominiums and also marine commercial and live/work facilities, the development maintains the fishing and marine background of the area. It has been recognized by the federal government as a model for sustainable building practices. The developers cleaned up the soil, recycled some of the buildings and utilized such advanced features as ground-source heat and passive solar design so that the building consumes 50 per cent less energy than conventional buildings.

At Shoal Point there is a helicopter landing pad control centre and a Flight Service Station which activates the strobe lights that indicate takeoffs and landings of the float planes. The Point can serve as your turnaround marker, just before you enter the Outer Harbour.

Paddle back the way you came, to the launch site in front of the Ocean Pointe Resort. If you wish a longer trip, you can now proceed west along past Pallastsis Point (also called Songhees Point) to West Bay (or go on the Upper Harbour marine trail to the Tillicum Bridge).

The Lekwungen people lived for over 4,000 years on southern Vancouver Island, on territory extending from Albert Head to Cordova Bay and including the San Juan Islands. Pallastsis Point was a gathering place for Songhees people and other visiting First Nations. "Pallastsis" in the Lekwungen (Songhees) language means "place of the cradle." When babies were old enough to walk, Songhees mothers would put their babies' cradles on the point to ensure long life. There was a reserve of Songhees people in this area for many years. A bridge called Indian Bridge (where the Johnson Street Bridge is today) connected the reserve to the city of Victoria. In 1911, as concern by "upright citizens" grew about having the reserve so close to the growing city, the reserve was relocated to the

We thought you otter know …
… how to tell the difference between river otters and sea otters.

Sea otters

- live along the northern Pacific coast
- stay close to shore and near beds of kelp
- use kelp for camouflage, for flotation when sleeping, and to anchor themselves from floating out to sea
- are one of the few animals that use tools: stones to crack shells open or pry them off rocks; may carry a favourite stone even when diving
- have wide, flat tails and long, webbed toes which form flippers
- use their whiskers like radar to find prey in muddy waters
- have thick fur that keeps them warm, as they have no blubber
- live from 8 to 12 years or more
- weigh 28 to 42 kg

- need to eat as much as ¼ of their weight in food every day
- often float in groups together

River otters

- live in most of the rivers of the world
- do not stay in the water as much as sea otters
- play and fish in the water but live in dens on shore
- need to eat as much as ¼ of their weight in food every day
- have a thick, ropelike tail they can use to stand upright
- have head and flippers similar to sea otters
- keep their fur very clean so it can trap air bubbles for warmth and buoyancy
- weigh up to 14 kg

northeast side of Esquimalt Harbour. Each native family was paid for their land, which was soon used for industrial purposes. Now, the area varies between industrial factories and shipworks north of the Johnson Street Bridge and high-end condos and the resort at the south end. At one time there was a military marine hospital and then an "insane asylum" from 1872 to 1878 in the point area, which was then called Hospital Point. A rock in the harbour in front of the place was called Hospital Rock, until it was blown up in 1914 to improve navigation safety. The cement forms that remain on the Point were the footings for a water tower for the

Sidney Roofing Company, one of the many industries that once were in the Songhees industrial reserve.

The Spirit of Lekwungen Nation totem pole was erected in 1994 at the beginning of the Commonwealth Games as a symbol of friendship between visiting nations. Concerns about its height impeding low flying aircraft resulted in it being cut into four pieces in 1997. Now two pieces are on the Point and two pieces are at the Esquimalt reserve.

Continue along the waterfront of the condominium complex toward West Bay. You will pass Mud Bay, Lime Bay and Coffin Island Point (really a peninsula). In the 1800s Coffin

Island was one of three islands used by the Songhees as a burial ground. The bodies were put in grave boxes with blankets and other personal articles, and some were then placed in small wooden houses. Mud Bay was separated from Lime Bay by a peninsula and was a frequent camping place for First Nations visiting the area. Lime Point, long ago, was a First Nations fortified village and later a burial ground. Both Lime Bay and Mud Bay were partially filled in when industry located along the shores of the harbour in the 1930s.

West Bay is the location of more floating homes and is home base for Harbour Ferries. The log pilings in the area are left over from an old booming grounds that held logs until they were needed in the sawmills that replaced the Songhees settlement. There is a restaurant here, and Canada's oldest licensed brew pub overlooks the West Bay Marina.

You may see some purple martins darting in and out of the bird houses, and river otters playing on the floating logs.

Beyond West Bay, you are looking at the Outer Harbour. In the distance you can see the Olympic Peninsula, with mountains rising over 2134 m.

Now retrace your marine trail back to the launch site, take your kayak out and enjoy a walk along West Song Way to stretch your legs or, having expended a fair amount of energy, indulge in some of the chocolates, sweets and ice creams that Victoria has in abundance as you look out at the harbour from the city perspective.

Water, water, every where,
And all the boards did shrink;
Water, water, every where,
Nor any drop to drink.

from The Rime of the Ancient Mariner, *by Samuel Taylor Coleridge (1772–1834)*

The sternwheeler Craigflower *taking tourists to see the reversing falls in The Gorge, ca. 1908. Photo courtesy City of Victoria Archives.*

A SHORT HISTORY OF THE GORGE AND PORTAGE INLET

I N THE TRADITIONS OF THE SONGHEES and the Kosapsom First Nations who inhabited the area around Portage Inlet and the Upper Victoria Harbour area, The Gorge Waterway had special meaning. For more than 5,000 years prior to European contact the area was used to collect and process shellfish. The descendants of the Songhees and the Kosapsom continue these traditions on the Esquimalt Reserve and the New Songhees Indian Reserve 1A, north of Tillicum Bridge and west of Craigflower Road.

History **continues on p. 148**

11 Upper Victoria Harbour, The Gorge Waterway and Portage Inlet

Difficulty Beginner conditions – low risk

Distances 4 nmi from Songhees Point to the Tillicum (Gorge) Bridge round trip.
Portage inlet is 1.2 nmi past the Tillicum Bridge, and depending on how far into the inlet you go, can be up to an additional 4 nmi round trip.

Durations 1.5–2 hours round trip to The Gorge waterfalls
3–3.5 hours round trip if you go through The Gorge into Portage Inlet.
Be aware of tides which may mean you cannot get back out through The Gorge under the Tillicum Bridge.
If you launch on the north side of the Tillicum Bridge at the Victoria Canoe and Kayak Club, it is approximately a two-hour trip to travel around all the inlets in the Portage Inlet at a leisurely pace. If you go up the Colquitz River, add at least another 45 minutes.

Charts 3415 Victoria Harbour, 1:6,000
3440 Race Rocks to D'Arcy Island, 1:40,000
Small-Craft Nautical Map Set A

Launching and take-out sites

Access to the Upper Harbour and Gorge Waters is slightly better than for the more built-up Inner Harbour area. The beach south of the Delta Ocean Pointe Resort on Songhees Point is still your best choice for direct access to the harbour. It is a short carry from the road to a sandy beach tucked beside the rocks of the point. If you wish to paddle on the north side of The Gorge tidal rapids and in Portage Inlet, there is an excellent launch site by the Victoria Canoe and Kayak Club (VCKC) off Gorge Road just west of Tillicum Road. The beach on the right is free for public use, but the dock is privately owned by VCKC, so ask permission before launching from it. The other access points are from the docks of the kayak rental businesses in the Upper Harbour. Phone ahead, as some will charge launching fees for non-renters. Contact information is listed in the resource section of this book.

Getting there

Songhees Point: From downtown Victoria take the Johnson Street Bridge ("Blue Bridge"), and after passing under the railway bridge on the Esquimalt side, turn left onto Tyee Road, which will then turn into Songhees Road. The launch point will be visible on your left below the highly visible totem pole.

Victoria Canoe and Kayak Club: From downtown Victoria, take Government Street north to its junction with Gorge Road (Highway 1A)/Hillside Avenue. Turn west onto Gorge Road and follow it for approximately 2.75 km. About 100 m after passing Tillicum Road, turn left into the VCKC parking lot.

Guide **continues on p. 149**

The Gorge was named for the physical character-istics of the land and river: a long, narrow waterway divided about midway between Portage Inlet and the Up-per Victoria Harbour by a narrowing of the river that cre-ated reversing waterfalls. The name Portage Inlet relates to the portage the First Nations made, using the present Portage Regional Park area, from the Inlet through to the present Thetis Cove area.

The Hudson's Bay Company directed one of its subsidiaries, the Puget Sound Agricultural Company, to establish farms in the area of Victoria. Craigflower, one of the most successful of these, was established at Maple Point, along The Gorge Waterway. These farms reduced the need for importing goods from other nations, helped create a more self-sufficient environment for the HBC and its employees, and fulfilled its obligations to Britain by supporting colonization. By increasing the number of colonists living and working in the towns and sur-rounding areas, Britain hoped to establish a firmer claim on Vancouver Island. The development in the 1880s of Gorge Road, extending north from Victoria, led to residential construction along The Gorge Waterway.

The Gorge area of Victoria's waterways was known as The Arm by the farming settlers who lived along its shores. Once Victoria's population increased and the citi-zens had time and money to enjoy recreational pursuits, the reversing falls became one of the most popular tourist attractions in the area. Engine-powered sternwheelers took tourists to see the rapids under the Tillicum Bridge, similar to the Harbour Ferries tours today. South of Tillicum Bridge was the scene of regattas, swimming competitions and diving.

History continues on p. 150

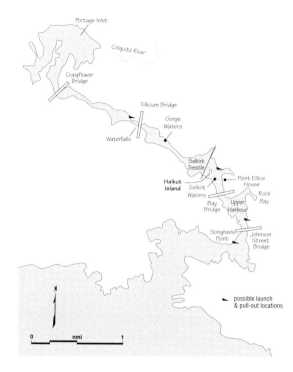

Portage Inlet

Colquitz River

Craigflower Bridge

Tillicum Bridge

Gorge Waters

Waterfalls

Selkirk Trestle

Halkut Island

Selkirk Waters

Point Ellice House

Rock Bay

Bay Bridge

Upper Harbour

Songhees Point

Johnson Street Bridge

➤ possible launch & pull-out locations

N

0   nmi   1

Parking

Free parking is available on the streets nearby the Delta Ocean Pointe Resort. Note that parking is free all day Sunday and for 2½–3½ hours Monday through Saturday. If you are launching from a rental location, inquire with the outfitter for your best option, but expect to have to pay at most locations.

Free parking is also available at the VCKC parking lot and on Gorge Road across the street.

Washrooms

Delta Ocean Pointe Resort is very kind in allowing use of their lower level washrooms, through the ground level café. Try not to track sand and water into their facility. Most of the rental locations have washroom facilities.

Paddling considerations

If you do not want to risk the reversing falls at Tillicum Bridge, launch on the north side of the bridge, at the beach beside the Victoria Canoe and Kayak Club, for a paddle in the Portage Inlet area.

The Upper Harbour, Selkirk Waters, Gorge Waters and Portage Inlet areas are ideal for kayaking. They are gen-

Guide continues on p. 151

Now, both The Gorge and Portage Inlet are sur-rounded by homes instead of farmland, but during the summer months many of the former recreation aspects have returned, with rowers, canoeists and kayakers frequenting the waterways. A yearly regatta, the Selkirk Waterfront Festival, is held in June with rowing races, dragon boat tours, musical performances and family food and fun. On the day after the festival, there is a Gorge cleanup, and each year volunteers pull out over two tonnes of garbage.

ᙍᖆ

The Gorge regatta, May 1890. Photo courtesy City of Victoria Archives.

Victoria Upper Harbour and "Blue Bridge"

erally well protected from wind and extreme weather, so your biggest hazards will be the large amount of other small-boat traffic, especially on busy weekends in the summer. Remember, unlike you, rowers are not looking forward as they paddle.

The reversing tidal rapids at the Tillicum Bridge are a great place to practise manoeuvring in currents, but should be avoided by most paddlers. Currents here can reach 8 knots, with strong whirlpools, eddies and standing waves. Careful timing is required to safely navigate through this area, and only experienced paddlers should attempt it.

The route

If you are launching at Songhees Point (Pallastsis Point), cross over to the east side of the harbour and paddle north toward the "Blue Bridge" (Johnson Street Bridge).

The majority of interesting buildings are on the east side of the waterway, since on the west side much of the landscape, for the first part of the trip, is taken up by industry and new housing developments. Of note, though, is the Point Hope Shipyard, which has been doing marine repair and shipbuilding since the late 1800s.

On your right you will see two empty old buildings, and after crossing under the bridge, the back of one more (the Janion Building, a hotel built in 1891). These are all owned by an elderly lady who, it is rumoured, will only sell them to the right person who is willing to restore them to their former style and purpose.

Where the Johnson Street Bridge now crosses the Upper Harbour, there was, in the late 1800s and early 1900s, a wooden bridge called the Indian Bridge because it led to the Songhees Reserve. In 1924, this was replaced by another wooden bridge. The present span is a bascule bridge which uses a counterweight of 707 tonnes to balance the 317-tonne opening span. It has two separate bascules, to accommodate both a railway and a highway section. The bridge was designed by Joseph Strauss, who also designed the Golden Gate Bridge in San Francisco, California. The blue paint was chosen in 1979 when the superstructure was repaired, because the oxides of the pigment in the paint are the same colour as the paint so that the colour fades very little. The bridge competed with Alicia Silverstone for a starring role in the movie *Excess Baggage*, filmed in 1996.

The Esquimalt & Nanaimo Railway (E&N) terminal is on the north side of the Johnson Street Bridge and uses the railway portion of the bridge to begin its journey up the Island to Courtenay. Originally this rail line was envisioned to be the western end of the Trans-Canada railway uniting Canada from east to west. In fact, British Columbia refused to join Confederation unless the province was connected with the eastern railway system. At the time of Confederation there were more people living on Vancouver Island than on the mainland, so Esquimalt was considered an appropriate end of the rail line. From the harbour the line was to run north to Seymour Narrows (north of Campbell River),

Log bridge over The Gorge waterfalls, ca. 1850s. Photo courtesy City of Victoria Archives.

where boats or bridges would take the trains across to the mainland.

By 1874 the rail line had still not been built and Prime Minister Sir John A. Macdonald undertook to persuade Robert Dunsmuir (a self-made millionaire) to finance it. It was to Dunsmuir's advantage to do this, since the train could then haul coal from his mines at Nanaimo to the port of Esquimalt. Finished in 1886, the track was extended into Victoria in 1888. In 1949 the E&N was the first railway in Canada to become completely diesel powered. Today, the line hauls some freight but is mainly operated as a tourist train by VIA Rail and owned by the CPR. Only 225 km long, this is the fourth shortest railway in Canada.

After Robert Dunsmuir made his millions, he built Craigdarroch Castle on the highest hill in Victoria to keep a promise to his wife to build her a castle when they immigrated to Canada. His son James built Hatley Park on Esquimalt Harbour, which for many years after the death of the Dunsmuirs was an officer training college and now houses Royal Roads University.

On the edge of what was, in the mid-1800s, called the Johnson Street Ravine, a Chinatown of shanty homes was built on stilts. Hundreds of Chinese immigrants arrived with Americans and Europeans in 1858 to seek their fortunes in the goldfields. When Chinese were recruited to work on the CPR in the 1880s, there were more Chinese than Caucasians in Victoria. Many also came as merchants and several were successful. Loo Gee Wing, for example, owned a boat fac-tory, a store, a laundry and hotel in Victoria and a theatre in Vancouver. However, as with the First Nations and black populations, they encountered more prejudice than acceptance. There was both federal and provincial legislation (such as the $50 head tax for Chinese immigrants that was instituted in 1885 after the completion of the railway, and the Exclusion Act of 1923) that excluded the Chinese from full participation in the developing economy. However, the middle class Victorians and the developers were more than willing to depend on them for their labour in their homes, businesses and railways. The area became a six-block labyrinth of shops, opium dens, courtyards, brothels, homes and gambling dens. One of the narrowest streets in Canada, barely five feet wide, Fan Tan Alley (fan tan is a gambling game) is still there today, to remind us of the former activities and culture that existed here.

Once one of the most populous of Canada's Chinatowns, the area is now defined by quiet streets where shops sell the usual Chinese tourist products. There are also several restaurants that provide a taste of another culture, and a lot of memories drift with incense in the air.

Still on the east side of the water, at Mermaid Wharf and Marina, there is a sculpture called Four Winds. It was made by both casting and freestyle sculpture by Chippewas artist Chris Johnson (Ice Bear) and represents "Indigenous expression about the future as foretold in messages carried by the winds."

Beside the sculpture and behind the Canoe Club Marina is an original brick building that was called the City Lights Building. Built in 1894, it housed the coal-fired generators that created the electricity for the streetlights in Victoria. After a $6 million renovation that retained its exterior brick and interior timber frame, the building is now the site of a popular restaurant and brew pub. Behind it is another old brick building that was occupied by the British Welding Company during early Victoria years.

As you paddle on, you can see, side by side, the brick and frame building that is now the Capital Iron Building, the location of the Victoria Roller Flour and Rice Mills when it was built in 1867; and the refurbished building housing Ocean River Sports. Rice, silk and tea were imported from China and brought into the harbour on clipper ships to be sold or processed at the mills and in the stores of the town. One of these clippers, the *Thermopylae*, was the only full-rigged sailing clipper ship to be registered in Victoria and was considered the prize of the fleet. Local farmers would also bring their wheat to the mill to be ground and sold. Both of these buildings have been restored to close to their original appearance. The use of the red brick here and in many of the waterfront downtown buildings is typical of the type of construction that occurred in the boom of 1886–92.

At Barclay Point and Rock Bay the dust and noise of a Lafarge cement processing plant adds to the industrial nature of what used to be the site of gracious homes and attractive, tree-lined streets. This plant also demonstrates that the landscape in the surrounding country is still covered with limestone rocks that can be used in the production of cement, just as it was in the area of Brentwood Bay/Tod Inlet in the 1800s. Try not to tip over in your kayak in this area: a giant storm drain empties a third of Victoria's total runoff into Rock Bay.

Continue paddling under the Bay Street Bridge and on toward a Harbour Ferries dock for the Point Ellice House Museum and Tearoom.

You are now in the Selkirk Waters, having left the Upper Harbour. The upper Selkirk Waters served as a log-booming grounds well into the mid-20th century. During the late 19th century the Pleasant Street area, where Peter O'Reilly and his family lived, became one of the most fashionable residential districts in Victoria. In 1868 O'Reilly bought an Italianate style house in Point Ellice that had been built in 1861. With a conservatory, rose gardens, croquet lawn and tennis courts, it was one of the most luxurious homes in the area. The family entertained extensively, as did their neighbours. The first lawn-tennis tournament in Victoria was played on Point Ellice courts. Kathleen O'Reilly was one of two O'Reilly daughters who were frequently wooed by such men as Captain Robert Scott (of Antarctica fame). She never married, however, and lived in the house until her death in 1945. Peter O'Reilly served the B.C. community in his original position as magistrate and then as a Member of the Legislative Assembly and as the Indian Reserve Commissioner. Members of the O'Reilly family lived in the family home until 1975 and throughout their lives were considered part

Does the ghost of Kathleen O'Reilly show visitors through her former home, Point Ellice House? Photo, ca. late 1800s, courtesy British Columbia Archives.

of the "upper class" of Victoria. It is said that Kathleen's ghost sometimes escorts visitors through the museum and tearoom that are now housed in the building and owned and operated by the Province of British Columbia and The Land Conservancy of British Columbia. Here you can also see Victoria's largest group of arbutus— evergreen trees with broad leaves and peeling bark that love the dry soil of the Gulf Islands and southern Vancouver Island.

Additional ghosts have also been reported at Point Ellice and are believed to be of the individuals who died in the collapse of the Point Ellice Bridge (where the present Bay Street Bridge is located). This accident, on

May 26, 1896, was the worst streetcar disaster in Canadian history, taking the lives of 55 men, women and children who were returning home from an afternoon picnic and celebration on the Esquimalt side. Some of the bodies of the accident victims were brought to the grounds of the Point Ellice House.

As you paddle onward, a large, noisy scrap iron operation can be seen and heard to your right on weekdays. Here you can see metal objects get lifted by magnets, consumed by giant machines and spit out as metal filings.

Also on your right you will see a small bay and the large, modern structure that is the B.C. Ministry of the

Purple martin wire sculpture at B.C. Environment building

Environment building. In front of it is a metal and wire sculpture of a purple martin bird in flight. Since purple martins eat their weight in bugs every day, they are a very efficient environmental machine for keeping the insect numbers low around the waterways.

Just south of the trestle bridge, you will find Halkett Island. At low tide there are rocks close to the surface in the surrounding waterways. The island indicated the boundary between two local tribes, and was used as a burial ground. In 1867 four boys who were playing there managed to start a large fire that burned many of the burial boxes and trees. In 1993 the island was returned to the Songhees, reversing the earlier assumed ownership by the settlers.

As you paddle under the Selkirk Trestle Bridge, many bicyclists may be racing over it. This bridge once was the route for the Galloping Goose train, so called for the waddle of the train's compartments as it went from Victoria, past Sooke, to Leechtown, where a gold mining settlement existed in the early 1920s. For a brief time there were more people in Leechtown than in Victoria, but after the gold ran out, the town, and the tracks, were abandoned. Now, the railbed has become the Galloping Goose Regional Trail, a bicycle and pedestrian pathway that extends 100 km from Sidney to Sooke, with an extension to Leechtown. The route is part of the Trans-Canada Trail and is used by more than 2,000 commuters a day.

First Nations canoe races below The Gorge waterfall, ca. 1870s. Photo courtesy City of Victoria Archives.

Continue along this tree-bordered waterway lined with homes, only a few of which show styles of an earlier age. At one time, Curtis Point, located just before the arched Tillicum Bridge, had a series of diving towers from 10 to 100 feet high and was used for swimming instruction and competitions. The cement footings still visible on the Point were from steps to access a float. It was here too that in the 1880s that a successful Chinese businessman, Loo Gee Wing, built a pavilion over top of a boathouse on the property. Local lore maintained that his concubines lived in small huts and some were said to have committed suicide off the Point. In the 1920s when cars became a means of transportation, the Point became a popular spot for a tourist auto camp with small cabins for people to holiday in.

It was in this area in 1858, during the first gold rush heyday, that The Gorge Waterway regattas began. They were initially held on July 4 to help the U.S. prospectors celebrate their Independence Day, but disapproving royalists moved the date to the Queen's birthday, May 24. In the 1870s, races from the Gorge Falls to Halkett Island and back involving the First Nations were included. Canoe races, often starting in the Inner Harbour and racing to the Gorge Falls, continued until after the Second World War. Swim races also took the three-mile route from the Inner Harbour to the waterfalls.

The next bridge you will come to is the Tillicum Bridge. This is the pres-

A 19th century painting of Craigflower Manor, school and outbuildings. Photo courtesy British Columbia Archives.

ent-day name for the bridge over the reversing falls at the narrowest point of The Gorge Waterway. The word Tillicum comes from First Nations language meaning "How do you do, friend?" James Yates, who owned large tracts of land in the area, and another landowner are said to have greeted each other this way whenever they met in the bridge area, and this led to the name. The original bridge in 1848 was five logs stretching across the falls as a way to get from Fort Victoria to a sawmill at Millstream on Esquimalt Harbour. This was followed by wooden structures in 1867 and 1882. In 1920, when automobile traffic was beginning to increase, the bridge was limited to "pedestrians and vehicles with a maximum weight

of 2½ tons traveling no faster than 3 mph." A steel bridge was built in the 1930s and the present structure in 1967.

Boaters have always had the same challenge you will face today at these small reversing falls, except that getting past this spot is even more difficult today than it was in 1908. Back then, there was a wooden walkway around the east side of the land so that canoes could be lined through The Gorge. Even so, a large rock in the middle of the narrows created an added challenge of a whirlpool at the southern side. This rock was used as part of special First Nations rites. It was said to be the home of Camosun, the spirit of a young girl turned to stone by the transformer Haylas. After a ritual cleansing, young braves would dive into the whirlpool water created by the rock to obtain special powers such as success in hunting. Clothes washed in the foam were believed to protect the wearers from drowning.

In 1960 associates of the Gorge Boat House, built to the south of the bridge, unaware or uncaring about the spiritual importance of the rock, took it upon themselves to dynamite it, blowing nearly a metre off its top.

With good timing, which requires accurate use of the tide tables, you can make it through to Portage Inlet, paddle around there and make it back. Otherwise you may get stuck on the wrong side of up to an 8-knot current.

Whether you decide to go through or go back and put in at the north side of the bridge another day, here is what you will see.

The Gorge Park lies on either side of the waterway, both north and south of the Tillicum Bridge. The Kinsmen Gorge Park is on the west side.

The Victoria Canoe and Kayak Club began in 1969 and is housed in a designated historic building. On its website there are tide tables for Tillicum Gorge which will help you gauge your passage through the waterfall area.

As you continue to paddle along the waterway, it may seem as if you are constantly coming to a dead-end. The narrow winding nature of the waterway leads to surprise views and a perception of an extended distance to get to the Inlet.

Garry oaks, which are found almost exclusively on the Gulf Islands and

Craigflower farmhouse and school as they look today

Vancouver Island, and arbutus trees hang over the waterways. Houses line the shore but only a few are of any heritage value.

When you see a bridge with a white building on either side, you are approaching Craigflower Bridge and park. Where Craigflower Manor is now situated there was once an ancient village of the Kosapsom people, who lived in the area for over 3,000 years. Purchase of the land was recorded in the treaties signed by James Douglas and the native people. This farm was one of four in the area started under the auspices of the Puget Sound Agricultural Company, a subsidiary of the Hudson's Bay Company. Building at the farm began in 1853, with a mill, brickworks, bakeshop and blacksmith shop as well as the farm barns and sheds. A two-storey school for the children of farm workers and neighbours was built on the east side of the river and joined by a bridge. The school was also used as accommodation for student lodgers and the teacher, and as a meeting hall and church. The men of the community used it also for scientific presentations and discussion. It is now the oldest standing school in western Canada.

After you leave the Craigflower area, you can paddle along to your left to Christie Point and into the bay leading to Portage Regional Park. The marshy Craigflower Creek to the southwest as you head toward Portage Park allows for a brief diversion. It was here that the natives used to portage their canoes as a shortcut to the

A tranquil bend in the bayou-like Colquitz River

Esquimalt harbour. Once out on the main water of the Inlet, you can see, high on the hill to the northwest, the industrial-size pipes that are a functional architectural feature of Victoria General Hospital. The red ones house the mechanisms for heating, the blue for air-conditioning, and the green for recycled air.

At high tide, if you paddle to the northeast part of the Inlet, you may wish to explore the Colquitz River. This will take you under the Admirals Road Bridge and past Cuthbert Holmes and Tillicum Parks and almost as far as the Tillicum Shopping Centre. The river banks, with their moss-covered logs and hanging moss on the trees, help give an appearance of paddling through a bayou with the prospect of seeing an alligator around the bend.

Paddling in the Portage Inlet, with all its little bays, is a pleasant route where you will glide by a pastoral landscape with more modest houses than along The Gorge Waterway. Portage Inlet is a designated bird sanctuary so it may be worthwhile to take your binoculars on this trip. It will take you about an hour and a half if you go to the end of each bay, and more if you explore the creeks and rivers. How long you take will be governed by whether you need to get back through The Gorge waterfalls.

Make your way back to your launch site or, if you are trying to get through The Gorge waterfalls during slack tide, paddle madly off in all directions.

Wherever you pull out your kayak and finish your trip, it is time to head into the old part of the city, walk down Government Street to #913 and indulge in an energy-replenishing Rogers chocolate. The chocolates are made according to recipes that have been in use since 1885 and therefore qualify as a necessary part of this historical tour.

The tide rises, the tide falls,
The twilight darkens, the curlew calls;
The little waves, with their soft, white hands,
Efface the footprints in the sands,
And the tide rises, the tide falls.

The Tide Rises, the Tide Falls,
by Henry Wadsworth Longfellow (1807–1882)

A SHORT HISTORY OF
THE SAANICH PENINSULA

THE SAANICH PENINSULA IS LONG AND NARROW, surrounded by Saanich Inlet, Sydney Channel and Satellite Channel. It is a major entry to Vancouver Island for both ferries and aircraft.

For thousands of years the Saanich (meaning "emerged" or "elevated") area was the winter home of the Coast Salish Tsartlip First Nations, where they hunted, fished and gathered food and plants. In the 1850s large amounts of Saanich land was purchased for the employees of the Hudson Bay Company by Chief Factor James Douglas (reportedly in exchange for 386 woolen blankets). The area became a valuable resource to Fort Victoria and the developing city, as it supplied much-needed fresh produce and dairy goods.

Today, the countryside is both urban and rural, with most of the land still devoted to agriculture much as it was during early settlement. When you drive along the country roads to reach Tod Inlet, you will often see roadside fruit and vegetable stands with a trusting "honesty box" for payment.

એ

12 Tod Inlet, Brentwood Bay and the Butchart Gardens

Difficulty Novice conditions – minimal risk

Distance 3 nmi from Brentwood Bay to the end of Tod Inlet round trip

Duration 1.5 hours round trip

Charts 3441 Haro Strait, Boundary Pass and Satellite Channel, 1:40,000
3462 Juan de Fuca Strait to Strait of Georgia, 1:80,000
Small-Craft Nautical Map Set B

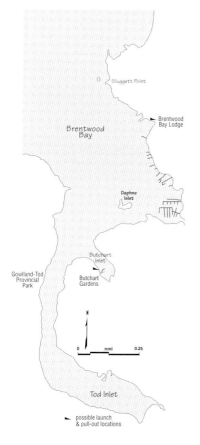

Launching and take-out site:
The Verdier Rotary Park, located just before the ferry dock at the end of Verdier Avenue, provides a gradual path down to a pebble and sand beach.

Getting there
From Victoria: Follow Highway 17 north until you reach Keating Cross Road. This is about 14 km from Hillside Avenue in Victoria. Turn left and follow Keating Cross Road for about 3 km until you reach West Saanich Road. Turn right and go 1.5 km to Verdier Avenue. Turn left and follow the road to its end, where you will see Verdier Rotary Park on your left.

From Swartz Bay Ferry Terminal: Follow Highway 17 south for about 7 km until you reach McTavish Road. Turn right and follow McTavish Road for 3 km until you reach West Saanich Road. Turn left and follow West Saanich Road for about 6 km until you reach Verdier Avenue. Turn right and follow until the end, where you will see Verdier Rotary Park on your left.

Parking
Along Verdier Avenue adjacent to Verdier Rotary Park.

Tod Inlet village and cement plant, ca. early 1900s. Photo courtesy Butchart Gardens.

Washrooms

There is a porta-potty close to the street at the top of Verdier Rotary Park. If you buy a pastry or coffee from the bakeshop at the Brentwood Bay Lodge and Spa you could use their washrooms. Gowlland-Tod Park at the end of Tod Inlet has outdoor toilets.

Paddling considerations

The Brentwood Bay/Tod Inlet area is ordinarily a sheltered and safe location for paddling, but like anywhere on the West Coast, conditions can change quickly. Be aware of winds from the north and northeast that could make it much more difficult to return to your launch site after leaving the shelter of Tod Inlet. The Mill Bay ferry, float planes, pleasure boats, divers and tour boats should also be kept in mind when paddling here.

The route

Put your boat in to the south of the Mill Bay ferry dock and paddle away from the village of Brentwood Bay. The town was originally named Sluggett after a settler by that name who lived in the area in 1876. In 1925 the name was changed to Brentwood after the English town of the same name. This town was the previous home of Robert Horne-Payne, who was president of the British Columbia Electric Company. Along with several other financiers, he also established the Consolidated Railway Company from the three electric interurban tram companies operating in Vancouver, New Westminster and Victoria. A oil-fired generator was built in the Brentwood area to produce some of the electricity for the line. It was this company that was involved in the Point Ellice streetcar disaster, and despite being cleared of fault (it was the city bridge that gave way), rapidly went into bankruptcy as a result of the accident. Horne-Payne and his partners raised more capital, chiefly

in England, and developed the B.C. Electric Railway Company, which ran the interurban lines for the next 64 years. The 40-km line from Deep Cove in Saanich to Victoria never had enough traffic to make it profitable, and it closed in 1924.

Immediately beside the launch site you will see a large luxurious lodge, the Brentwood Bay Lodge and Spa. It was built on the site of the Brentwood Bay Inn and opened in 2004 with a coveted status as one of only three exclusive hotels in Canada to have membership in the Small Luxury Hotels of the World. Now, instead of a genteel cup of tea in the tea room of the old Inn, you can indulge in gourmet meals and other luxuries. The resort offers their guests such activities as a tour

The Brentwood Bay Lodge and Spa, 2005

Tod Inlet, Brentwood Bay and the Butchart Gardens – 165

Brentwood Bay, ca. early 1900s. Photo courtesy British Columbia Archives.

of the inlet with a marine biologist, diving and, yes, kayaking.

The mouth of the Saanich Inlet that you see to your far right as you leave the beach is North America's southernmost fjord. Because only the top two hundred feet of water is affected by tidal exchange, the lower water layers in the deep inlets in this area have been undisturbed for thousands of years. This marine environment gives rise to unique marine life. There are thousand-year-old glass sponges, and other sponges that are 12 feet across—the largest ever recorded. There are wolf eels, rockfish and rare, six-gilled sharks. Even if you are not diving, you will be able to see some of this amazing marine life from your kayak. Along the shore there are gigantic sea stars of various colours, and watch out—the giant Pacific octopus

lurks in these waters! Although most grow to only about 45 kg, one captured near Victoria in 1967 weighed 70 kg and measured 7.5 m between the tips of opposite arms—big enough to capsize your kayak if one of those long arms were to reach out and . . .

On the opposite shore is a modern-day gravel and cement factory and Mill Bay, the terminus of the Brentwood Bay to Mill Bay ferry route, which is described as "the most beautiful shortcut in B.C."

Head southwest across the water to the mouth of Tod Inlet. The area was called Snictel—"place of the blue grouse"—by the First Nations people who lived here. Five archaeological sites have been discovered, and in the middens remains of humpback whales, rare Pacific oysters and fish, crab and waterfowl bones indicate

Portland cement plant at Tod Inlet, ca. early 1900s. Photo courtesy Butchart Gardens.

why this area was chosen for habitation.

The name Tod Inlet was given to recognize the contributions of John Tod, who for 40 years worked for the Hudson's Bay Company, rising from a clerk posted to isolated places, to the senior officer at Fort Kamloops. When Tod retired he started a trend that continues today in Victoria, by choosing to live in Oak Bay, where his home still stands. After his lengthy service to the HBC, he was appointed a member of the Vancouver Island Legislative Council and later a Justice of the Peace and a member of the first Provincial Assembly. Part of his reputation, however, has to do with what, for the time, was considered numerous relationships and marriages (reputedly at least seven) and children (ten). At least some of these children were from the common practice of HBC employees having relations with First Nations women ("country wives") and then leaving them and their mutually produced children behind when they moved on to another fort.

A small sign on the right bank indicates the beginning of the Gowlland-Tod Provincial Park, which, together with the Butchart Gardens property, surrounds Tod Inlet. The 1200-hectare park was created after the 1994 Commonwealth Games in Victoria to help protect the remaining natural environments close to the city.

On the west side of the Inlet there are two white buoys. These mark the places where, in 2000, some 1,800 eelgrass plants were placed to help with marine rehabilitation of the area and provide improved habitat for fish.

Tod Inlet was used for boat access to the remote community of the same name which existed at the mouth of the Tod River when the Portland Cement Company was active during the early 1900s. There were about 20 small homes for families, and tents and bunkhouses for the men, many of whom were Chinese workers who had previously worked on building railways in Canada and the U.S.

At the south end of Tod Inlet, there is now a dinghy dock and picnic site as part of the Gowlland-Tod Provincial Park, with a washroom and short trails around the area. This is a good spot to have a wander about and see some of the remains of the former factory that made cement until 1916 and remained open, producing tiles and flowerpots into the 1950s. There is a small concrete building from the plant (near the washroom) and pilings from the old dock. In the distance (inside the property of Butchart Gardens) can be seen one of the kiln chimneys of the cement factory. In the fall, there are apples on many of the trees, which have now grown wild. If you bring a bag for picking, you can make pie from some of them when you get home.

Go close to shore on your way back out of the Inlet and you will often see very large sea stars and shells on the ocean floor. Round the corner and enter Butchart Inlet. This small bay and the gardens surrounding it are named after the Butchart family, who have spent a century nurturing a spectacular garden. The dock at the side of the inlet is for securing boats, seaplanes and kayaks while their owners visit the gardens. In the sum-mer there is often an attendant at the small kiosk to take your admission. Unfortunately, there are no discounts just because you arrived by water. If no one is there, you can ring a buzzer. There is also a video security system that lets the main office know who is in the dock area.

In 1902 Robert Butchart purchased the 90 hectares and the Saanich Lime Company that was on it. He rapidly duplicated his original success in establishing the Portland Cement Company in Ontario and by 1904 had established a successful busi-ness in cement production on the West Coast. He was the first to put cement in jute bags instead of barrels and contributed to the construction of roads, sidewalks and buildings in Victoria and other coastal cities by the production of cement. His wife, Jenny Butchart, was equally talented. She was an artist and an equestrian, as well as a qualified chemist who helped her husband with the testing and quality control of the cement in the early days of production.

You can see part of a Japanese gar-den facing the dock and inlet. It was the first garden Jenny Butchart built when she decided to begin to beautify the surroundings of her home. This area was farthest away from the dust and noise of the cement plant. By 1908 the quarry had run out of lime-stone and Jenny conceived the idea of a sunken garden to transform the unattractive pit that was left. Horse and cart transported topsoil from neighbouring land, and her husband provided workers to help develop the landscape. In 1921 the sunken garden was completed. It was followed by the Rose Garden, the Italian garden and other flower areas. Today, over 1,000,000 bedding plants of over 700 varieties are planted each year, so there is continuous bloom from spring to fall.

The Butchart family have been leaders in many fields. The Butchart Gardens developed the seed so the Tibetan blue poppy could grow in B.C., and over the years other unique flowers have been developed as well. Jenny was one of the first women to drive an electric car when they were introduced, and Robert was among the first 20 people in the Victoria area to have a gasoline-powered car. Both the Butcharts were gracious in sharing their home, Benvenuto (Welcome), and gardens with the rich and famous and the general public alike. Robert was made a Freeman of the City of Vic-

toria in 1928, and Jenny was Victoria's Citizen of the Year in 1931. Their son, Ian, was made a member of the Order of Canada in 1992. Over the years, programs such as weekend evening fireworks, Christmas lights and the symphony in the gardens have been added. Centennial celebrations in 2004 marked the 100th year that the Butcharts, their children and now their grandchildren have maintained the gardens as a family-run business, continuing the tradition of innovation in garden development and programs, not to mention the cordial welcome extended daily to more than a million visitors every year.

Back in your kayak and out of the inlet on your return to the launch site, you can make a leisurely tour past the small islet of Daphne and the boats at the marina and government wharf,

The Butchart sunken garden today. Photo courtesy Butchart Gardens.

The Butchart sunken garden, ca. 1912. Photo courtesy Butchart Gardens.

trying to avoid looking at the sprawling, monotonous development on the hill above the Bay.

If you want a longer paddle, go past the ferry wharf and the waterfront of Brentwood Bay village and continue around the point. This area is on the Tsartlip Reserve and is private property; there is a fee to use the boat launch. Return to the launch beach and perhaps a specialty massage at the Lodge to help your muscles be ready for your next adventure.

Once more upon the waters! yet once more!
And the waves bound beneath me as a steed
That knows his rider.

from Childe Harold,
by Lord Byron (1788–1824)

Early Historical Events in the Vancouver and Victoria Area

Past 3,000 years: Coast Salish peoples live in the Vancouver and Victoria areas.

1778: English Captain James Cook visits Nootka Sound, and trade in sea otter pelts begins.

1789: The Spanish open a naval base at Nootka Sound and assert sovereignty over the coastline.

1790: England and Spain sign Nootka Convention whereby Spain cedes its claim to the coast.

1791: Spanish captain Narvaez charts areas around the mouth of the Fraser and Point Grey, Burrard Inlet and Howe Sound.

1792: Captain George Vancouver charts the coastline, names the Gulf of Georgia after the reigning king, and explores Burrard Inlet and Howe Sound area as far as Jervis Inlet.

1792: Spanish Captains Galiano and Valdes explore along the length Indian Arm.

1808: Simon Fraser reaches mouth of Fraser River.

1843: Fort Victoria is established on Vancouver Island.

1846: Oregon treaty is signed, establishing 49th parallel as border between U.S. and colony of British Columbia.

1849: Vancouver Island is granted to the Hudson's Bay Company, with James Douglas as Chief Factor.

1849: First Nations given equal rights to own land.

1852: Large quantities of coal are found at Nanaimo, Vancouver Island.

1858: The discovery of gold on the Fraser River is followed by a "gold rush" influx of miners.

1858: The mainland is recognized as the Colony of British Columbia, and James Douglas, who was Governor of Vancouver Island, becomes governor of both.

1859: Royal Navy Captain Richards begins charting the Burrard Inlet to establish military reserves to forestall U.S. expansion.

1859: Capital of British Columbia colony is moved from Derby near Fort Langley to Queensborough, later named New Westminster, to establish better defences.

1860: New Westminster becomes incorporated, the first municipality west of Ontario to do so.

1862: One third of First Nations people in B.C. die in a smallpox epidemic.

1866: Victoria becomes the capital of British Columbia when the colonies of Vancouver Island and British Columbia are united.

1867: Canadian Confederation.

1868: Purchase of land by Ladner brothers in Delta starts a permanent settlement there.

1870: (Vancouver) townsite is named Granville as Gastown and smaller settlements merge.

1870: First European settles on Bowen Island.

1871: British Columbia becomes a province.

1876: Indian Act is created, establishing band councils and Indian agents as intermediaries between First Nations and the rest of Canadian citizens.

1884: Laws forbidding traditional potlatch ceremonies are enacted. Resistance occurs by First Nations who express belief in hereditary title. Residential schools are developed.

1886: Fire destroys most of the newly incorporated city of Vancouver.

1887: Arrival of the first transcontinental passenger train in Vancouver from Montreal (preceded in 1886 by arrival of a train at Port Moody).

1891: Incorporation of the area from Indian Arm to Howe Sound as District of North Vancouver.

1897: Klondike gold rush.

1898: The great fire in New Westminster destroys most of the town.

1900: First ferry service to North Vancouver established, followed in 1909 by service between Vancouver and West Vancouver.

1907: City of North Vancouver incorporated, separate from the District of North Vancouver.

1909: Request denied when First Nations ask King Edward VII to have aboriginal title be decided by the Privy Council. Federal government under Wilfred Laurier supports recognition of aboriginal rights.

1912: Incorporation of West Vancouver separate from North Vancouver.

1914: First World War breaks out in Europe.

1915: Formation of the Allied Tribes of British Columbia to define title and treaties.

Useful Contacts

Websites worth visiting

BC Dive & Kayak, Vancouver:
www.bcdive.com

BC Ferries: **www.bcferries.com**

Bowen Island Sea Kayak:
www.bowenislandkayaking.com

Canadian Coast Guard:
www.boatingsafety.gc.ca

Charts and Marine Publications:
www.charts.gc.ca

Deep Cove Canoe and Kayak, North Vancouver:
www.deepcovekayak.com

Ecomarine Ocean Kayak Centre, Vancouver: **www.ecomarine.com**

English Bay Info:
www.englishbay.com

Environment Canada Vancouver weather: **http://weatheroffice.ec.gc.ca/forecast/city_e.html?yvr**

Jericho Sailing Centre:
www.jsca.bc.ca

Kat Kam of English Bay:
www.katkam.ca

Kaymaran Adventure Tours, Ladner:
www.kaymarantours.com or
www.ladneroutdoorstore.com

The Land Conservancy:
www.conservancy.bc.ca

Mountain Equipment Co-op, Vancouver and North Vancouver:
www.mec.ca

North Fraser River Port Authority:
www.nfpa.ca

Ocean River Sports, Victoria:
www.oceanriver.com

Pacific Paddle Sports, Victoria:
www.gotpaddle.net

Paddling.net: **www.paddling.net**

Recreation Equipment Inc., Seattle:
www.rei.com

Sea Kayak Association of B.C.:
www.skabc.org

Sea Kayak Instruction and Leadership Systems: **www.skils.ca**

Sea Kayak magazine:
www.seakayakermag.com

Vancouver Archives:
http://city.vancouver.bc.ca/cty-clerk/archives

Vancouver Library Special Collections, digital archival photos:
http://vpl.vancouver.bc.ca/branches/LibrarySquare/spe/photos/photoagree.html

Vancouver Parks:
http://city.vancouver.bc.ca/parks

Victoria Canoe & Kayak Club:
www.vckc.ca

Wave Length magazine:
www.wavelengthmagazine.com

West Vancouver Archives:
www.wvma.net

Western Canoe & Kayak, Abbotsford:
www.westerncanoe.com

Where to rent

Renting kayaks can be the most economical and convenient way to get on the water. We have compiled a list of the outfitters located near the routes detailed in this book. Be sure to call before you go, for business hours, reservation policies, and boat availability. It is also a good idea to ask what is included. Rentals should include all Coast Guard required gear, and will often also include a spare paddle and paddle float. Clothing and dry bags are usually up to you. If you plan on transporting the boat(s) to another location, find out what is available to help you with this, and what you need to bring of your own. Most outfitters will require a credit card security deposit as well as photo ID to show that the card really is yours. Solo renters will need to prove they can do a self-rescue.

Lower Mainland

BC Dive and Kayak
Rentals, lessons, tours, sales
1695 West 4th Avenue
Vancouver, B.C.
604-732-1344
www.bcdive.com
Year round, 10–6
Rentals: single and double ocean
  kayaks

Bowen Island Sea Kayak
Rentals, lessons, tours, sales
1213 Main Street
Bowen Island, B.C.
on the water
604-947-9266

www.bowenislandkayaking.com
April 1 to October 31, 8:30–dusk
Rentals: single and double ocean
  kayaks
Tours: half and full day tours
Special events: Around Bowen Race

Deep Cove Canoe and Kayak
Rentals, tours, lessons, sales
2156 Banbury Road.
North Vancouver, B.C.
on the water
604-929-2268
www.deepcovekayak.com
April–mid-October, dawn to dusk
Rentals: single and double ocean
  kayaks, canoes
Tours: local tours from half day to
  overnight; moonlight paddles.
Special events: Tuesday Night
  Paddle Races
Special rates: cheaper mid-week
  rentals; season pass; take a boat
  home for the winter

Ecomarine Ocean Kayak Centre
Rentals, tours, lessons, sales
1668 Duranleau Street, Granville
  Island, Vancouver, B.C.
on the water
604-689-7575, 1-888-425-2925
www.ecomarine.com
Open all year, hours vary
Rentals: single and double ocean
  kayaks
Tours: local half day tours;
  moonlight paddles
Special events: monthly free
  evening seminars; annual kayak
  marathon; demo days
Special rates: 2 for 1 Tuesdays
  (applies to two-hour rental rates);
  season pass

Ecomarine Jericho
Rentals, lessons
1300 Discovery Street
Vancouver, B.C.
on the water (in the Jericho
   Sailing Centre)
604-222-3565
www.ecomarine.com
May–September, 9–dusk
Special rates: 2 for 1 Tuesdays
   (applies to two-hour rental rates);
   season pass

Kaymaran Adventure Tours
Rentals, lessons, tours, sales
4860 Chisholm Street
Ladner, B.C.
on the water
604-946-5070
www.kaymarantours.com
7 days a week spring to early fall;
   closed Mondays and Tuesdays
   late fall to spring
Regular hours spring/summer
   Mon–Sun 9–5; fall/winter
   Wed–Sat 9–5, Sun 11–5
Rentals: single and double plastic
   ocean kayaks, canoes
Tours: half day local tours

Mountain Equipment Co-op
Rentals, sales
130 West Broadway,
   Vancouver, B.C.
604-872-7858
www.mec.ca
Open all year, hours vary
Rentals: single and double ocean
   kayaks, whitewater kayaks,
   canoes ·
Special events: check website

Rocky Point Kayak Rental
Rentals, lessons, tours
2715 Esplanade Avenue,

Port Moody, B.C.
on the water
604-619-WATER (2837)
www.rockypointkayak.com
April–September, 9–dusk
Rentals: single and double ocean
   kayaks
Special rates: discounts on shoul-
   der-season rentals
Tours: half day local guided trips

Victoria and Brentwood Bay

Brentwood Bay Lodge, Spa and Marina
Rentals, ecotours
849 Verdier Avenue,
   Brentwood Bay, B.C.
on the water
250-652-3151 marina
   250-544-2079 main lodge
www.brentwoodbaylodge.com
Open all year; Mar 1–Oct 31, 8–6
Rentals: single and double kayaks
Tours: fall/winter weather
   dependent

Gorge Kayaking Centre
Rentals, tours, lessons
2940 Jutland Road, Victoria, B.C
on the water
250-380-4668
Seasonal, call in advance during
   off season
Rentals: single and double kayaks
Tours: guided tours can be arranged

Island Boat Rentals (Harbour Rentals)
Rentals, tours
450 Swift Street, Victoria, B.C.
on the water
250-995-1661

www.greatpacificadventures.com
May–October, 10–6
Rentals: single and double kayak
rentals
Tours: can be arranged

Marine Adventure Gallery at Shoal
Point
Rentals, sales
21 Dallas Road, Victoria, B.C.
on the water
250-361-3684
www.marineadventuregallery.com
Rentals from April–November;
retail year-round
Rentals: single and double ocean
kayaks

Ocean River Sports
Rentals, lessons, tours, sales
1824 Store Street, Victoria, B.C.
on the water
250-381-4233 or 1-800-909-4233
www.oceanriver.com

Pacific Paddle Sports
Rentals, lessons, tours, sales
575 Pembroke Street, Victoria, B.C.
250-361-9365 or 1-877-921-9365
www.gotpaddle.net
Open all year, hours vary
Rentals: single and double kayaks,
whitewater kayaks, canoes
Tours: single and multi-day tours

Bibliography

Armitage, D. *Burrard Inlet: A History*. Madeira Park, B.C.: Harbour Publishing, 2001

Barefoot, K. *Victoria: Secrets of the City*. Vancouver, B.C.: Arsenal Pulp Press, 2000

Blake, D. *BC Trivia*. Edmonton, Alberta: Lone Pine Publishing, 1992

Bowen Island Chamber of Commerce. *Bowen Island Guide*. 2004

Brownell, B. *Amazing Otters*. Washington, D.C.: National Geographic Society, 1989

Burkinshaw, R. K. *False Creek: History, Images and Research Sources*. Vancouver, B.C.: City of Vancouver Archives, 1984

Cherrington, J. A. *The Fraser Valley: A History*. Madeira Park, B.C.: Harbour Publishing, 1992

Davis, C. *The Greater Vancouver Book*. Canmore, Alberta: Altitude Publishing, 1998

Delta Museum and Archives. *Harvesting the Fraser*. Altona, Manitoba: Friesens, 2003

Francis, D. *The Encyclopedia of British Columbia*. Madeira Park, B.C.: Harbour Publishing, 2000

Grant, P., Dickson, L. *The Stanley Park Companion*. Winlaw, B.C.: Bluefield Books, 2003

Greater Vancouver Regional District. *Deas Island Regional Park, Belcarra Regional Park* (pamphlets)

Gourley, C. *Island in the Creek: The Granville Island Story*. Madeira Park, B.C.: Harbour Publishing, 1988

Hill, K. and Hill, G. *Victoria and Vancouver Island: A Personal Tour of an Almost Perfect Eden*. Guilford, Connecticut: The Globe Pequot Press, 2001

Hooper, G.F. *Esquimalt & Nanaimo Railway* (pamphlet). Mileposts Citizens Association to Save the Environment

Howard, I. *Bowen Island 1872–1972*. Bowen Island, B.C.: Bowen Island Historians, 1973

Indian Arm Natural History Group. *Indian Arm: Natural and Cultural History* (pamphlet)

Jepson, T. *Rough Guide to Vancouver*. London, U.K.: Rough Guide, 2001

Mackie, J. & Reeder, S. *Vancouver the Unknown City*. Vancouver, B.C.: Arsenal Pulp Press, 2003

MacDonald, C., Drake, D., Doerksen, J., Cotton, M. *Between Forest and Sea: Memories of Belcarra*. Burnaby, B.C.: Belcarra Historical Group, Simon Fraser University, 1998

McCullough, M. *Granville Island: An Urban Oasis*. Vancouver, B.C.: Canada Mortgage & Housing, 1998

Minaker, D. *Next to The Gorge: A History of the Neighbourhood Bound by Tillicum, Burnside & Harriet Roads and the Gorge Waterway, 1852–1996*. Victoria, B.C.: Desktop Publishing Ltd., 1996

Minaker, D. *The Gorge of Summers Gone: A History of Victoria's Inland Waterway*. Victoria, B.C.: Desktop Publishing Ltd., 1998

Morgan, R. and Disher, E. *Victoria Then and Now*. Vancouver, B.C.: Bodima Books, 1977

Ramsey, B. *A Place of Excellence*. Corporation of the District of West Vancouver, 1986

Rose, R. *Talls & Flats, Ovals and Squats: A History of Early Salmon Canning in Delta 1871–1913*. Delta, B.C.: Delta Museum and Archives and British Columbia Heritage Trust, 1986

Snyders, T. and O'Rourke, J. *Namely Vancouver*. Vancouver, B.C.: Arsenal Pulp Press, 2001

Sparks, D. and Border, M. Inwood, D. (Ed.). *Echoes Across the Inlet*. Cloverdale, B.C.: Deep Cove and Area Heritage Association, Friesen & Sons Ltd., 1989

Steele, R. M. *The First 100 Years: An Illustrated Celebration*. Vancouver Board of Parks and Recreation, 1988

Swanson, D. *Welcome to the World of Otters*. Vancouver, B.C.: Whitecap Books, 1997

Vogel, A. and Wyse, D. *Vancouver: A History in Pictures*. Canmore, Alberta: Altitude Publishing, 1993

Walker, E. *Street Names of Vancouver*. Vancouver, B.C.: Vancouver Historical Society, 1999

Ward, R. *Echoes of Empire: Victoria & Its Remarkable Buildings*. Madeira Park, B.C.: Harbour Publishing, 1996

White, H. (Ed.). *Raincoast Chronicles #19.* Vancouver, B.C.: Harbour Press, 2003

Wood, D. *Waterfront Odyssey.* British Columbia Magazine, Fall 2000

Wynn, G. and Oke, T. (Eds.), *Vancouver and Its Region.* Vancouver, B.C.: UBC Press, 2003

Websites

www.city.victoria.bc.cityhall/departments
www.riverwork.org
www.nfpa.ca
www.frpa.ca
www.portvancouver.com
www.nwheritage.org
www.DeepCoveHeritage.com
www.wvma.net
www.yvr.ca
www.bcferries.com
www.britishcolumbia.com
www.butchartgardens.com
www.city.vancouver.bc.ca/parks
www.collections.ic.gc/craigflower
www.fairmont.com

Newspapers

Vancouver Sun

Fralic, S. April 30, 2004. "Form meets function in new building"

Pemberton, K. September 13, 2004. "New towers at SFU are a 'tragedy,' architect says"

Penner, D. August 11, 2004. "City gets power to repel boat boarders"

Young, K. October 25, 2003. "Inuit sculptures widely popular"

The Vancouver Courier

Carrigg, D. July 25, 2004. "Squamish standing pat on valuable Kits property"

Hughes, F. July 25, 2004. "Luxury lodge an ideal launching pad for eco-marine activities"

MacNeill, I. July 14, 2004. "On the Waterfront"

Additional Reading

General Sea Kayaking

Alderson, D. *Sea Kayaker's Savvy Paddler: More than 500 Tips for Better Paddling.* Camden, Maine: Ragged Mountain Press, 2001

Backlund, G. and Grey, P. *Easykayaking Basics: A Paddling Handbook For the Pacific Northwest.* Madeira Park, B.C.: Harbour Publishing, 2004

Dowd, J. *Sea Kayaking: A Manual for Long Distance Touring.* Vancouver, B.C.: Greystone Books, 2004

Hansen, J. *Complete Sea Kayak Touring.* Camden, Maine: Ragged Mountain Press, 1998

Hutchinson, D. *The Complete Book of Sea Kayaking.* Guilford, Connecticut: The Globe Pequot Press, 1995

Johnson, S. *The Complete Sea Kayaker's Handbook.* Camden, Maine: Ragged Mountain Press, 2002

Navigation

Birch, D. *Fundamentals of Sea Kayak Navigation.* Guilford, Connecticut: The Globe Pequot Press, 1999

Moyer, L. *Sea Kayak Navigation Simplified.* Mukilteo, Washington: Alpen Book Press, 2001

Safety

Alderson, D. and Pardy, M. *Sea Kayaker Magazine's Handbook of Safety and Rescue.* Camden, Maine: Ragged Mountain Press, 2003

Broze, M. and Gronseth, G. *Sea Kayaker Magazine's Deep Trouble: True Stories and Their Lessons from Sea Kayaker Magazine.* Camden, Maine: International Marine/Ragged Mountain Press, 1997

First Aid

Christensen, A. *Mis*Adventure: Rise to the Challenge.* Vancouver, B.C.: Wilderness Alert Publishing, 2003

Weather

Environment Canada. *West Coast Marine Weather Hazards Manual.* West Vancouver, B.C.: Gordon Soules Publishing, 1999

Lang, O. *Living with the Weather along the British Columbia Coast: The Veil of Chaos.* West Vancouver, B.C.: Gordon Soules Publishing, 2003

Lang, O. *The Wind Came All Ways: A Quest to Understand the Winds, Waves, and Weather in the Georgia Basin.* West Vancouver, B.C.: Gordon Soules Publishing, 1999

Route Guides

Snowden, M. *Sea Kayak: The Gulf Islands.* Surrey, B.C.: Rocky Mountain Books, 2004

Stedham, G. *The Vancouver Paddler: Canoeing and Kayaking in Southwestern British Columbia.* Coquitlam, B.C.: Glen Stedham Publishing, 1999

Float Plans

A float plan is an essential part of any kayak outing. It is a record of when, where and with whom you will be paddling, when you expect to be back, and other information important to rescuers should an emergency occur. If you should not return on time this may be the only way a rescue is started and will make it much easier for rescuers to locate and assist you. It can be as simple as orally telling a partner or relative your plans for the day, or it can be as formal as a document that all members of the group fill out, leave with someone they trust, and bring along a copy in case of an emergency.

If you are renting a kayak, most outfitters will ask for your destination, return time, and an emergency contact number. Make sure to fill this information in, as the outfitter will be the first to notice if you have not returned as expected. If you are paddling independently, it is best to fill in a more formal float plan and leave it with someone you trust. Identify the local agency that should be contacted for a search and rescue. Make photocopies for everyone in your group. If an incident should occur, a written record will help ensure the group sticks to its plan. It is good to keep your copy of the plan attached to your boat at all times. In the unlikely event that you get separated from your boat, the float plan will provide rescuers valuable information on your possible whereabouts. Once you have completed your trip, don't forget to inform everyone with whom you left your float plan of your safe return. Should you fall behind schedule and not be able to make your designated return time, every effort must be made to inform the people with whom you left your float plan to avoid any unnecessary rescue attempts.

An example of a written float plan appears on the two sides of the next page. Simply cut along the handy dashed line to remove the float plan for photocopying at whatever size you prefer.

Float Plan

Date:_____Destination:_____

Latest return date, time:_____

In emergency, please contact:_____

_____

Group members:
Group leaders:_____

_____

Name_____Age ____Phone_____
   Boat type, colours_____

Name_____Age ____Phone_____
   Boat type, colours_____

Name_____Age ____Phone_____
   Boat type, colours_____

Name_____Age ___ Phone_____
   Boat type, colours_____

Name_____Age ____Phone_____
   Boat type, colours_____

Name_____Age ____Phone_____
   Boat type, colours_____

Name_____Age ____Phone_____
   Boat type, colours_____

Name_____Age ____Phone_____
   Boat type, colours_____

Basic trip plan:

Launch site, time:_____

    drop of vehicle:_____

Route description:_____

_____

_____

_____

Take-out site, time:_____

    pick up vehicle:_____

Alternative route:_____

_____

_____

_____

Communication gear:

        cell phone ❑   VHF radio ❑

Cell phone numbers:_____

_____

VHF channels monitored:_____

    daily times monitored_____

Search & rescue gear:

flares ❑   number and type_____

strobes ❑   dye marker ❑   flashlights ❑   signal mirrors ❑   light sticks ❑

Notes:

Gear Checklist

Coast Guard required gear:
- ❑ secure buoyancy
- ❑ Coast Guard approved PFD
- ❑ paddle
- ❑ regulation 15 m buoyant heaving line
- ❑ pump with float
- ❑ whistle (attached to your PFD)

Gear you should always take:
- ❑ float plan (also left with relatives or friends)
- ❑ spray skirt
- ❑ spare paddle
- ❑ paddle float
- ❑ dry bags
- ❑ chart of the area
- ❑ local tide and current tables
- ❑ emergency contact phone numbers for the area
- ❑ rain jacket or paddling jacket
- ❑ extra warm clothes (wool or fleece) in a drybag
- ❑ protective footwear
- ❑ sun hat/rain hat
- ❑ sunglasses with retainer
- ❑ sunscreen and lip balm
- ❑ at least two litres of water per person
- ❑ lunch and some high-energy snacks
- ❑ toilet paper
- ❑ garbage bags
- ❑ compass
- ❑ waterproof watch
- ❑ waterproof headlamp
- ❑ knife
- ❑ cell phone in waterproof case
- ❑ VHF radio in waterproof case
- ❑ spare batteries
- ❑ first aid kit
- ❑ spare blanket
- ❑ repair kit
  - ○ duct tape
  - ○ five-minute epoxy
  - ○ rudder cable and crimps
  - ○ 4 mm accessory cord
  - ○ Leatherman or other multitool
  - ○ lighter
  - ○ Aquaseal
  - ○ wire
  - ○ Zap straps
  - ○ spare nuts and bolts to fit your equipment

Gear that's nice to have:
- ❑ sponge
- ❑ gloves or pogies
- ❑ deck bag
- ❑ chart case
- ❑ cockpit cover
- ❑ paddle leash
- ❑ deck-mounted compass
- ❑ camera and film or spare digital media
- ❑ waterproof camera case
- ❑ waterproof binoculars
- ❑ GPS
- ❑ rescue sling
- ❑ waterproof notebook
- ❑ chemical light sticks
- ❑ bum pad
- ❑ kite or sail
- ❑ fishing gear and licence
- ❑ change of footwear

Gear for more advanced trips:
- ❑ 360-degree white light for paddling after dusk
- ❑ flares (minimum 3)
- ❑ dye marker
- ❑ white rescue strobe light
- ❑ signal mirror
- ❑ coaming tow line
- ❑ sea anchor
- ❑ wetsuit or drysuit
- ❑ extra food and water

Index

More Great B.C. Books

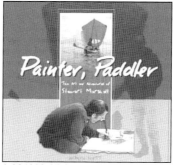

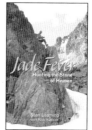

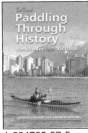
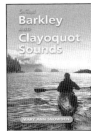
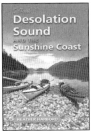